Investigating Our Language

John Richmond
and
Helen Savva

Edward Arnold

Preface

© John Richmond & Helen Savva 1983

First published 1983
by Edward Arnold (Publishers) Ltd
41 Bedford Square, London WC1B 3DQ

British Library Cataloguing in Publication Data
Richmond, John
  Investigating our Language.
  1. English language
  I. Title II. Savva, Helen
  428   PE1112

ISBN 0-7131-0610-7

Filmset in 11/12 Compugraphic (Century) by RDL., 26 Mulgrave Road, Sutton, Surrey and Printed by Thomson Litho Ltd, East Kilbride, Scotland

To the student

In the title of this book, the most important word may be the middle one. The language we investigate belongs to all of us. It is a human invention, and it helps to make us what we are. Also, it is an important tool for understanding the world, for living in the world, and for changing the world. So it is worth investigating.

We hope you find the information in this book interesting. We hope it makes you think. Don't feel that you have to agree automatically with us. The book is not meant to provide you with answers, but to help you to question. None of the activities in the book leads to a right answer. We hope that, by doing the activities, you will find your own answers. You don't have to stick to our activities word for word. Change them if you need to. But don't change them just to make them easier.

Most of all, use the book as a starting-point, not as a finishing-point. If the book leads you on to other ideas and other activities, you will have used it well.

To the teacher

This book takes its tone from its title. We hope that it will encourage an exploratory, questioning approach to language. We have not even tried to cover all the areas we think important, but have concentrated on a few topics in some depth.

The text is frequently interrupted by suggestions for activities. These activities are varied. For instance, the writing activities suggested include story writing, critical writing on literature, surveys, simple linguistic analyses of varieties of English, playscripts, summaries, commentary on transcripts of talk. The talking activities suggested include interviewing, formal group discussion, pair discussion, collaborative talk over specific projects, improvised drama. The activities vary in their difficulty, too, and in the length of time they would take to complete. Most of them require no more equipment than is available in a normal classroom. Some require the use of a cassette tape-recorder. A few presume that a library and reference books are available. But the book is quite usable without those facilities. Many of the activities can be done in one or two lessons without complex preparation; others require organization and planning over a series of lessons.

We have deliberately obscured the distinction between language and literature. For example, in Chapter 4 we use the Bible story of the prodigal son as the subject of linguistic analysis, while in Chapter 5 we illustrate a historical argument about language by using extracts from West African literature.

When we began writing, we envisaged that the book would be used by fourth- or fifth-year secondary classes, principally in English, and linking with any examinations which require course-work. Since then, other audiences have been suggested, slightly older or slightly younger. We have used the phrase 'school or college' occasionally in the text, to cover the possibility that the book might be used in sixth-form colleges or in further education.

We are not going to offer detailed advice about *how* the book should be used, whether with whole classes or with smaller groups, or about how closely the teacher should guide the learner's involvement with the book. The book's ideal function, it seems to us, would be as the centre of a programme of work which incorporated the teacher's and students' own materials and ideas, and where activities were taken up which went beyond the immediate scope of the book itself.

We have thought at length about the order of the chapters. There are obvious logical arguments for having a chapter on the origins of language first. On the other hand, the obvious logical order is not necessarily the best psychological order. Chapter 1 carries a fair load of information which may be unfamiliar to many learners. So the teacher or learner should not feel obliged to use the chapters in the order presented here.

JOHN RICHMOND
HELEN SAVVA

Acknowledgements

To Stephen Eyers, Alex McLeod, Mike Rosen, Susanna Steele and Geoffrey Thornton, for conversations, specific advice and continual encouragement.

To Shirley Clarke, Angela Coley, Angela Copeland, Sandra Herridge, Julie Roberts and Joe Steele Rosen, for allowing us to use talk and writing.

To Ray Booth and Andy Paterson, for taking photographs.

Illustrations by Martin Pitts.

The Publishers' thanks are also due to the following for permission to reproduce copyright material in this book:

Dover Publications Inc for 'Saylan' taken from *Jamaican Song and Story* by Jekyll, New York 1966; Faber and Faber Limited for 'The Storm' from *The Collected Poems of Theodore Roethke*; John Farquharson Ltd for extracts from Katzner: *Languages of the World*; 'The Gallis Pole' by Huddie Ledbetter, new material John A & Alan Lomax © 1959 Folkways Music Publishers Inc. assigned to Kensington Music Limited. International Copyright secured. All rights reserved; Mrs Helga Greene for an extract from Raymond Chandler: *Farewell my Lovely*; William Heinemann Ltd for an extract from Chinua Achebe: *Things Fall Apart* and John Steinbeck: *Of Mice and Men*; Bill Naughton for an extract from *One Small Boy*; Penguin Books Ltd for 'Botany Bay', 'Jim Jones' and 'The Buffalo' from Roy Palmer (ed): *A Touch on the Times*; Sangster's Book Stores Ltd for Louise Bennett 'Colonization in Reverse'; Mary Yost Associates Inc for an extract from Sembene Ousmane: *God's Bits of Wood* and Warner Bros Music Limited for the lyrics of Ian Dury 'My Old Man'.

The Publishers also wish to thank the following for permission to reproduce copyright photographs:

Tom Smillie: cover tl, & pp. 20l, 36 & 43; Mansell Collection: cover tr, & pp. 11t&b, 38r, 61l&r, 63, 69, 70, 71b, 72, 74tac, 75t, 76, 79, 83 & 84; B.B.C: cover bl & p. 34; Henry Grant: cover br & p. 47l; Catherine Shakespeare Lane: pp. 1, 24 & 25l; National Film Archive: pp. 5 (United Artists), 39, 60 (E.M.I.) & 87; The Museum of Mankind/BM: p. 14t; Barnaby's Picture Library: pp. 14b (Peter Larsen), 25r (Mervyn Rees), 47r (Juliette Radom) & 88 (A.W. Besley); Musée de L'Homme: p. 18t; Anthony McAvoy: pp. 20r & 46; Terry Williams: p. 26; *The Observer Magazine*: pp. 28 & 29; United States Travel Service: p. 30t&b; Edward Arnold Ltd: p. 30 l&r; G.L.C. Photo Library: p. 32; Ray Booth: p. 33; The Victoria & Albert Museum: p. 51; Jazz Journal International: p. 54; Polydor Recording Artists: p. 55; The Bible Society: p. 56; Drawing by Seymour photographed from Dickens: The Pickwick Papers: p. 58; Western Mail & Echo Ltd. Cardiff: pp. 67 & 68; Mary Evans Picture Library: pp. 71t & 75b; Sangsters Book Stores, Kingston, Jamaica: p. 77; Heinemann Educational Books: pp. 80 (George Hallett) & 82; Illustrated London News: p. 85r.

Contents

1

Where does our language come from?

This book is about language. As well as that, this book uses language. The two sentences you've read (two and a half now) are language.

That's the trouble with a book like this. You might have a book about the town where you live, or your favourite game, or the Second World War, or you might have a book of stories which you enjoy. Books like that use language to tell you something about the outside world, whether it's a place, or an activity, or a piece of history, or personal experience. The difficulty with a book *about* language is that, in a way, it's talking about itself. So we must be careful not to get cross-eyed when we use language to describe language.

The most important question to ask about language is: what is it? Like a lot of quite difficult questions, that question seems at first sight to be ridiculously easy.

Everyone knows what language is. It's obvious. Just to show yourself how easy it is, try this activity:

Think, talk, or write about the question: *what is language*? If you're talking with a friend or a group, a cassette tape-recorder is a useful way of recording what you say. Its disadvantages are that some people are shy of it, and if you're not used to it you can spend more time worrying about whether it's working properly than thinking about what you're saying. Having someone in the group who's prepared to take notes is another way of recording what is said. If you're writing, we leave the length up to you. If you really don't know how much to write, say half a page. You might find, once you've written that, that you'll want to write more.

Two important messages before we go any further.
1) In future, every time we suggest an activity for you to do, that activity will appear inside a frame, like the one above.
2) Some of the activities will ask you to write, and some will ask you to talk. Some will involve both. If we suggest an activity, or ask a question, without definitely saying 'Write!' or 'Talk!', that means you can do either, or both. Occasionally, it may be enough just to think.

How did you get on with the first activity? Easy or not? Anyhow, here's our *attempt* to say what language is. (The

1

question: *what is language?* is an open question, which means there's no one right answer to it.)

Language is words. Words carry meaning. People use language when they're talking, listening, writing, reading, or thinking. The main job of language is giving meaning and getting meaning. Giving meaning and getting meaning is *communication.* The main job of language (but not the only one) is communication.

That's one answer. Like all answers, it has certain things wrong with it. For instance, you could easily forget, if you stuck to that answer, that there are forms of communication which don't use words at all, or use words only partly. Language is not necessarily the same thing as communication.

Make a list of forms of communication which don't use words, or use them only partly. Describe some of the ways in which these kinds of communication work. Two examples you might start off with are *numbers* and *traffic lights*.

Schools and colleges are very serious about reading and writing. They do a lot of both. Here you are reading this. But there would be no reading or writing if there hadn't been talking in the first place. Although people have been reading and writing for a long time, they have been talking for much, much longer. Every day of our lives, we are surrounded by talk and talkers. That brings us to the next activity.

Give an answer to the question: *what is talk?*

The question: *what is talk?* is another open question, so the answer you've just given is one of many possible answers. Here's our possible answer.

Just as writing is arranging shapes on the page, so talking is arranging sounds in the air. People have been making and arranging sounds, and giving ideas with

them and getting ideas from them, for the last three million years (maybe longer). That makes writing, not much more than 5000 years old, a very new invention indeed.

Although more people on the earth can now write than ever before, they talk much, much more than they write. If you were to go about for one normal day with a tape-recorder round your neck, and then sit down and write out every word you had said, you would cover dozens, maybe hundreds, of sides of paper. Of course, it would depend on how talkative you are, and on the kinds of things you had been doing that day. But you would certainly find that it would take you a lot longer than one day to write out the words that it had taken you one day to say.

---

1) Talk into a tape-recorder for two minutes, or tape a conversation with a friend; then, either individually or together, transcribe (write out) what you have taped onto paper. Make sure that you take down everything on the tape exactly as you have said it, including *ums* and *ers*, pauses, stammers and false starts.
2) Think about and make a list of any of the differences you notice between your speech as you have transcribed it, and your normal writing.

Languages which aren't written down

There are many languages in the world which are not written down at all. People like us, whose language is written down, sometimes think that for this reason our language is better than languages which are not written down. Often, we go on from there to think that we are better, or more intelligent, or more civilized than speakers of unwritten languages. All this is nonsense. Writing is a very useful and excellent tool, but it does not make a certain language *better*, nor does it make the people who speak that language *better*. Making a telephone call is not a *worse* thing to do than writing a letter. It is different, and used for different purposes. Similarly, languages which do not use writing are not *worse* than languages which do.

Language and communication

People who study language are called *linguists*. Almost all linguists agree that all the languages ever studied are equally good at doing their job. We've already said that the main job of language is communication.

Now, if you're going to communicate, either by talking or by writing, you need to make the sounds or the shapes which the people you want to communicate with will understand. There needs to be agreement. We have to agree that *head* means that hard round thing with eyes, nose, mouth, ears and hair which sits on the top of our necks. If one person understands that *head* means that hard round thing, but another person understands that *head* means *those two long pointed things with five toes each which stand at the bottom of our legs*, the two people will soon get confused if they talk to each other about *heads*.

How did we begin to talk?

Nobody knows exactly how, why or when language first happened. But it's a very interesting question, and so plenty of people have thought about it, and put forward theories (ideas of their own) to try to answer the question. Nobody knows, for instance, whether language first happened in only one place, and spread over the whole earth as people spread, or whether it happened in several different places separately. There are three or four thousand different languages spoken in the world today, and it seems amazing that they should all have come from one beginning. But nobody knows.

What we have to say about the earliest beginnings of language is a mixture of two or three theories. These theories, like all the others, leave many unanswered questions. Much of them is guesswork. Still, it's better to have some ideas about a question than none at all, as long as we don't get big-headed about those ideas. So here they are.

Language came to exist because people who lived close together, and saw each other a lot, began to use the same sounds to mean the same things. As time passed, they used more and more sounds, arranged the sounds in more and more different ways, so they could talk to each other about more and more things. Of course, they only talked about the things which interested them, and which they knew about, just as we do. They had no word for *television* or *motorway*, but they must have had words for things which mattered to them, which we can't even imagine today.

This may sound very straightforward, but it's important to remember the time-scale involved. People who study the ancient past of the earth now think that we can look back five or six million years and say, 'Here is the creature which has become modern man and woman'. We can look back three million years and say, 'People have been communicating by making sounds with their voices and mouths for this long'. But it may be only 40,000 years since we have definitely used speech in the way we understand it today. In that enormous length of time between three million and 40,000 years ago, several things happened.

Homo Erectus, or *Upright Man*, lived in Africa a million and a half years ago. He didn't just pop up one morning. *Homo Erectus* is the name given to a stage in the development, or *evolution*, of men and women. That evolution led to *Homo Sapiens* (*Wise Man*, or *Man who can Reason with Himself*) about half a million years ago, and then to *Homo Sapiens Sapiens* (fully modern human beings) about 50,000 years ago.

The use of the word *Man* here is very unfortunate, because of course there were just as many women about as men. English hasn't yet got a proper word which means *all human beings, men and women*. If we use the word *Man* to mean *everybody*, we make *women* invisible. So let's talk about *people* instead.

Homo Erectus was developing the right organs in the throat and mouth for making a variety of sounds. As people did this, they learnt how to use those organs more and more efficiently. And the more they did that, the more the organs developed.

Meanwhile, people began to find that some of their grunts, howls and calls could be used to sound like certain things which they wanted them to mean. Suppose, at the time of early *Homo Erectus*, there was a common bird which hooted like an owl. People had got tired of flapping their arms or going out to point at one of the birds whenever they wanted to describe it. They found that if they made a sound like *Hoooo!*, other people knew that they meant a particular kind of bird, because the bird made that sound too. You can imagine that they could do the same with bears and wolves and other animals.

1) Invent a new word for the English language, which would mean *all human beings, men and women* and could take the place of *Man* in the section above. The word must not favour one sex more than the other, but it might be useful if it were somehow connected with words you know already. Invent another, shorter word, which would mean *he or she.* Explain how you came to decide on your new words.
2) Try to describe simple objects to a friend without using words. You can only use signs and gestures. If you succeed in doing this, try to communicate a more complicated message without the use of words.

A true story, from modern times, might help us to think more clearly about *Homo Erectus* learning to speak.

Victor, the wild boy

In 1797, a wild boy was seen living naked and free in woods in the region of Aveyron in France. No one knows for certain how the boy came to be living in this wild state, enduring extreme cold in winter and surviving on nuts and root vegetables which he ate raw.

He was captured twice, and escaped both times. The second time, in July 1799, an old widow looked after him for eight days before he got away. On 8 January 1800, the boy entered the village of Saint-Sernin and walked into the workshop of a man called Vidal.

The boy was 12 or 13 years old, but was only 4½ feet tall. He had brown straight hair, dark eyes and a light complexion. His face was marked by several scars and traces of smallpox. Slashed across his throat there was a thick scar. He appeared to be deaf and dumb.

At first the boy was sent to an orphanage. He became known as the Wild Boy of Aveyron, since he had no other name. Later, he was moved to the town of Rodez and then to Paris. In Paris he attracted the interest of some famous doctors of the time. When others wanted to abandon the boy as an idiot, a young doctor called Itard agreed to try to educate him.

The boy lived with Dr Itard for the next five years of his life. He was given the name Victor and he made good progress. He learnt some social manners, to show affection and gratitude, to read and write simple sentences.

Dr Itard was a patient and devoted teacher. He worked out very clever programmes to help Victor's development and they both achieved a great deal. However, Victor failed to learn to speak and at last Dr Itard decided that Victor was incurably dumb.

This story was made into a film called *L'Enfant Sauvage* (*The Wild Boy*), directed by Francois Truffaut. It can be hired for your school or college.

---

1) Invent the first part of the story of the wild boy. How did he come to be living alone and wild in the woods? How did he survive?

2) When the boy was found, he seemed to have no language. Is it possible to think and make decisions without language? You might discuss this question in a group, and perhaps write down your findings.

3) Write a story about trying to make a relationship with a person who for some reason cannot talk as easily as you can. Possible reasons: the person might have had a stroke, which has left him or her unable to speak; the person might have been born deaf and dumb; the person has a very bad stammer.

You need to talk to organize

Imitating animal sounds was a big step forward for *Homo Erectus*. But people

5

soon found (*soon* might mean only about half a million years) that there was a limit to the number of things they could say with this kind of language. There are plenty of things which don't make any noise at all, so you can't imitate them. There are some things which you can't even touch, like *sky* or *sun*, but which are so important that you really want to talk about them.

People's lives were hard. Their food came either from gathering and eating the plants, roots and berries which grew wild around them, or from hunting. As people lived together in groups or tribes, they found that it was easier if they did the difficult and dangerous jobs together. So together they hunted and killed wild mammoths and other animals, pulled down trees for their fires, moved rocks which lay in the entrances of caves. If you're doing any work which involves more than one person, it's a good thing to be organized. Organization needs com-

munication. If the work you're doing is hard physical labour, you'll probably make grunting noises while you're doing it. Slowly, people found that the grunts they were making in any case could be used to organize the work. What started as *Uh!* might develop into a word meaning *Push!* What started as *Gih!* might become a word meaning *Kill!* People began to have words for doing things as well as for naming things.

Imagine some more sounds which might have started as grunts or sighs or yells, and developed into words with meaning. Don't worry that you're only guessing, and that *Homo Erectus* wouldn't have spoken in modern English. Write the list down like this:

1) Uh! . . . . Puh! . . . . Push!
2) Gih! . . . . Kih! . . . . Kill!
3) . . . . .

Deciding what means what

As *Homo Erectus* got closer to becoming *Homo Sapiens*, people began to agree together that certain sounds they could all make with their mouths and throats *would mean* certain things which existed and which they wanted to talk about. There was not necessarily any reason why the sound and the thing *should* be connected, as there had been with the bird or with *Kill*! The only reason why the sound and the thing *were* connected was that people had decided that they *would be*. Their brains and eyes and mouths and throats had all agreed together that this would happen. This agreement meant that people could go on to name as many things as they could make different sounds for.

As these possibilities became clearer, people's brains asked their mouths, tongues and throats to do increasingly clever tricks, to jump about faster, to make smaller and more exact distinctions between sounds so that more words could be used and understood separately. The more the mouth, tongue and throat practised, the more skilful they became.

By the time *Homo Erectus* had deveoped into *Homo Sapiens*, people could use some kind of speech to communicate with others. Unless we invent the time-machine, we shall never know what this speech sounded like. Was there more than one kind of *Homo Sapiens* speech at the very beginning? As well as saying things like 'I want to eat', did *Homo Sapiens* ask questions like 'If that is sky up there, who made it?'?

We need to be very careful, talking about the ancient past in this way. It's easy to imagine *Homo Erectus* waking up one morning and deciding to do all these wonderful things with language. Actually, it took so long for these things to happen that an average human lifetime today, about 70 years, is like half a second by comparison with how long it took. Also, most what happened to *Homo Erectus* in developing into *Homo Sapiens* was sub-conscious, which means people didn't know what was happening as it was happening. Millions of individual developing men and women lived and died without knowing the tiny part they were playing in the long process.

---

1) For those who enjoy science fiction: write an account of a time-machine journey to the distant past. You meet men and women who are just learning to use language. Describe their life, their surroundings, your adventures, your attempts to talk to them. What does their language sound like?

2) Earlier, when we described *Homo Erectus* imitating a bird, we were using a theory which has been called the *Bow-Wow theory*. The example about *Gih!* becoming *Kill!* uses a theory which has been called the *Heave-Ho theory*. Invent a theory of your own, different from these two, which tries to explain how people began to talk.

3) At this point, you may feel overloaded with information. Since we're about half-way through the chapter, it's a good place to stop and look back. You might find it handy to make a list of the topics we've thought about, or even to write a summary (say about a page) of what has been said.

Where did *Homo Erectus* live?

Homo Erectus, we have said, first lived in Africa. Over a million years ago groups of *Erectus* men and women spread north-wards, crossing the strip of land which joins Africa to Asia, and then moving east and west. Remains of *Homo Erectus* have been found in China, in several parts of Europe including France and Spain, on the island of Java, as well as in our birthplace of Africa. Hundreds of thousands of years passed. Nobody knows exactly when men and women reached America and Austra-lia. It is most likely that this happened between 100,000 and 10,000 years ago,

The early migrations of *Homo Erectus*

when the last ice age lowered the level of the sea by up to 400 feet. Then, the eastern tip of Russia was joined to Alaska by a bridge of land, and groups of wandering hunters and food-gatherers walked across, and began to move downward through America.

The first Australians were unique. They must have got there by sailing. The amount of sea to cross would not have been as much as today; but 20,000 years ago, maybe in dugout canoes, on purpose or by accident, men and women crossed 60 miles of sea and found Australia. The five continents we know today—Africa, Asia, Europe, America and Australia—were populated.

The slow-motion language explosion

The passing of thousands of years, and the spreading of people over the earth, meant that languages changed and multiplied. A good example of this is a language which was spoken by a people living in eastern Europe over 6000 years ago—sometime before 4000 BC. Some of those people travelled eastwards to the areas which are now Iran, Pakistan and northwest India. Others travelled west and south to the areas which are now Italy and Greece. Others travelled north-west to Germany and Scandinavia.

The language of the eastward travellers developed into Persian and Sanskrit. Nobody speaks Sanskrit today, but nearly all the modern languages of Pakistan and India come from it. The language of the westward travellers developed into Greek and Latin. Millions of people still speak Greek today, although it has changed a good deal since it was first spoken. No one speaks Latin any more, but it is the source language of French, Spanish, Italian, Portuguese and Roumanian, five great national languages, and of several other languages spoken by smaller groups of people.

Sanskrit

अस्ति हस्तिनापुरे कर्पूरविलासो नाम रजकः । तस्य गर्दे-
भो ऽतिभारवाहनाद्दुर्बलो मुमूर्षुरिवाभवत् । ततस्तेन रज-
केनासौ व्याघ्रचर्मणा प्रच्छाद्यारण्यसमीपे सस्यक्षेत्रे मोचितः ।
ततो दूराद्वलोक्य व्याघ्रबुद्ध्या क्षेत्रपतयः सत्वरं पलायन्ते । स
च सुखेन सस्यं चरति । अथैकदा केनापि सस्यरक्षकेण धूसर-
कम्बलकृततनुत्राणेन धनुष्कारादं सज्जीकृत्यायतनकायेनैकान्ते
स्थितम् । तं च दूरे दृष्ट्वा गर्दभः पुष्टाङ्गो गर्दभीयमिति मत्वा
शब्दं कुर्वांस्तदभिमुखं धावितः । ततस्तेन सस्यरक्षकेण गर्द-
भो ऽयमिति ज्ञात्वा लीलयैव व्यापादितः ।

In Hastinapura there was a washerman named Vilasa. His donkey
was near death, having become weak from carrying excessive
burdens. So the washerman covered him with a tiger-skin and
turned him loose in a cornfield near a forest. The owners of the
field, seeing him from a distance, fled away in haste, under the
notion that he was a tiger. Then a certain corn guard, having
covered his body with a gray blanket, and having made ready
his bow and arrows, crouched down in a secluded spot. Then the
donkey, having grown plump from eating, spied him at a distance,
and supposing him to be a she-donkey, trotted up to him braying.
The corn guard, discovering him to be only a donkey, killed him
with ease.

—*The Donkey in the Tiger-Skin*, from the *Hitopadeśa*

Persian

یارم چو قدح بدست گیرد   بازار بتان شکست گیرد
هر کس که بدید چشم او گفت   کو محتسبی که مست گیرد
در بحر فتاده‌ام چو ماهی   تا یار مرا بشست گیرد
در پایش فتاده‌ام بزاری   آیا بود آنکه دست گیرد
خرّم دل آنکه همچو حافظ   جامی ز می الست گیرد

When my Beloved the cup in hand taketh
The market of lovely ones slack demand taketh.

Every one saith, who her tipsy eye seëth
"Where is a shrieve, that this fair firebrand taketh?"

I, like a fish, in the ocean am fallen,
Till me with the hook yonder Friend to land taketh.

Lo, at her feet in lament am I fallen,
Till the Beloved me by the hand taketh.

Happy his heart who, like Hafiz, a goblet
Of wine of the Prime Fore-eternal's brand taketh.

—HAFIZ, *Cup in Hand*

Greek

CLASSICAL GREEK

φίλοι, κακῶν μὲν ὅστις ἔμπειρος κυρεῖ,
ἐπίσταται βροτοῖσιν ὡς ὅταν κλύδων
κακῶν ἐπέλθῃ πάντα δειμαίνειν φιλεῖ·
ὅταν δ' ὁ δαίμων εὐροῇ, πεποιθέναι
τὸν αὐτὸν αἰεὶ δαίμον' οὐριεῖν τύχην.
ἐμοὶ γὰρ ἤδη πάντα μὲν φόβου πλέα
ἐν ὄμμασιν τἀνταῖα φαίνεται θεῶν,
βοᾷ δ' ἐν ὠσὶ κέλαδος οὐ παιώνιος·
τοία κακῶν ἔκπληξις ἐκφοβεῖ φρένας.

My friends, whoever's wise in ways of evil
Knows how, when a flood of evil comes,
Everything we grow to fear; but when
A god our voyage gladdens, we believe
Always that fortune's never-changing wind
Will blow. As my eyes behold all things
As fearful visitations of the gods,
So my ears already ring with cureless songs:
Thus consternation terrifies my sense.
—AESCHYLUS, *The Persians*

Latin

Quae potest homini esse polito delectatio, cum aut homo
imbecillus a valentissima bestia laniatur aut praeclara bestia
venabulo transverberatur? quae tamen, si videnda sunt, saepe
vidisti; neque nos, qui haec spectamus, quicquam novi vidimus.
Extremus elephantorum dies fuit. In quo admiratio magna vulgi
atquae turbae, delectatio nulla exstitit; quin etiam misericordia
quaedam consecuta est atque opinio eius modi, esse quamdam
illi beluae cum genere humano societatem.

What pleasure can it give a cultivated man to watch some poor
fellow being torn to pieces by a powerful beast or a superb beast
being pierced with a hunting spear? Even were such things worth
looking at, you've seen them many times, and we saw nothing
new this time. The last day was devoted to the elephants. The
vulgar populace was enthusiastic, but there was no pleasure in it;
indeed, the show provoked some sort of compassion, a feeling
that there is some kinship between this great beast and human-
kind.

—CICERO, *Letters to Friends*

1) Remind yourself of what it was like in primary school when you were learning to write. Copy the Sanskrit, Persian or Greek as accurately as you can. You've come a long way, since it was as hard to write English as it is to write Sanskrit now!

2) How many different languages are spoken or written by people in your class or group? Collect all the information you can, by asking people to say and/or write down a few sentences of any language they know, other than English. Some people will be able to speak other languages but not write them; some will be able to do both. Organize the results of your survey as clearly as you can. You could ask people whether they speak a language very well, quite well or only a little. You could give them sample sentences of English to translate. You could ask them where and how they learnt, and when they speak, their other language.

3) You may be someone yourself who's lucky enough to be able to speak and/or write more than one language. If you are, you probably learnt one language as a baby (your mother-tongue) and the other(s) later on. What was it like, learning to speak your second (or even third) language? Tell the other members of your group.

Where English came from

From the language of the travellers to Germany and Scandinavia there developed German, Norwegian, Swedish, Danish, Dutch—and English. The Anglo-Saxons invaded Britain between AD 450 and 700. The Anglo-Saxons were people who came from northern Germany and parts of Denmark, and they brought their language with them. After a long struggle, the Anglo-Saxons conquered most of what is now England, and the people who had been living there before them had either to accept that they were beaten, or retreat to the westerly and northerly parts of Britain—Wales, Cornwall and Scotland. So the language of the Anglo-Saxons became Old English, though there were several different dialects of the language spoken in different parts of the country.

Strange as it may seem, then, there are connections between English and, say, Persian, which is spoken by over 20 million people in Iran and five million people in Afghanistan. The Persian word for *month* is *mah*; for *mother, madar*; for *new, nau*; for *three, se*.

There are many more connections between languages which are more closely related than English and Persian. The language of the Anglo-Saxons who stayed at home, and didn't invade Britain, and the language of the other tribes living around them, developed into German. For a while Old English and Old German were nearly the same language, and today there are still many words in the two languages which are exactly the same or very similar, such as *hammer/Hammer, hunger/Hunger, man/Mann, son/Sohn, mother/Mutter, to have/haben, garden/Garten, to kiss/küssen*.

So English is one of a large family of more than 50 languages, spoken by nearly 2000 million people all over the earth, and this family can be traced back 6000 years to a single language spoken by a people somewhere in eastern Europe. That language and people are known as Indo-European, because they spread to India and Europe, but we know only a very little about them.

Here is the English word *new* in 20 other Indo-European languages:

Welsh: newydd	Gaelic: nua
Portuguese: novo	Italian: nuovo
Dutch: nieuw	Icelandic: nýr
Czech: nový	Roumanian: nou
Lithuanian: naujas	Armenian: nor
French: nouveau	Spanish: nuevo
Latin: novus	German: neu
Swedish: ny	Polish: nowy
Greek: neos	Russian: novy
Persian: nau	Sanskrit: nava

Try to get hold of some foreign-language dictionaries. You'll probably find Armenian or Sanskrit hard to come by, so stick to French, German, Italian or Spanish. If you can only get one or two dictionaries, the exercise is still worth doing. Take some common English words, and see how they translate into the other languages. Quite often, you'll find an obvious connection with one or two of the other languages, but not with all of them. Sometimes, as with *new*, the word is similar in all the languages you look at. Your list might start like this:

English	French	German	Italian	Spanish
mother	mère	Mutter	madre	madre
hundred	cent	hundert	cento	cien
love	aimer	lieben	amare	amar

Drawing and counting came before writing

We have already said that writing was invented over 5000 years ago, so far as we know, and that writing is a very new idea compared to speech. However, people were making marks on solid surfaces long before they were writing, in two particularly important ways.

The first was cave painting. By the time *Homo Erectus* had completely given way to modern human beings, 40,000 years ago, the earth was in the middle of the last ice age. So far as Europe was concerned, this meant that the north polar region had got bigger and bigger, and had travelled down over Scandinavia, with ice covering what is now Germany and France, and even getting as far as Spain. So most of Europe was a very cold place to live, as cold as it is to live in Greenland today. We think of caves as being dark, chilly places, but if you get right inside them, they are quite warm. Not only that, but the temperature in most caves stays the same all the year round. So you don't freeze at night, and you don't freeze in winter. Very convenient. Certainly, it's pitch dark in caves, but men and women had learnt to use fire a long time before this.

Cave painting

People lived in caves in France, Spain and elsewhere for over 30,000 years, until after the end of the ice age, when the snows receded to the north, and warmth came back to the earth. In some of those caves it's still possible to see paintings done by those people. Animals are the most common subjects of the paintings—birds, fish, or the great woolly mammoths that the people hunted for food.

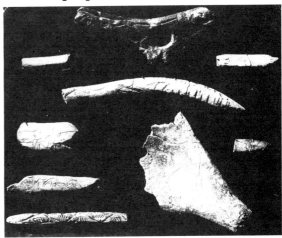
Bone markings

11

The second very early example of making marks on solid surfaces is the scratching of lines or dots on bones. From about 30,000 years ago, in many different parts of the world, people began to engrave lines or dots in organized ways on bones. Nobody today is quite sure what the lines and dots meant. They might have been a kind of calendar, or a way of marking off the phases of the moon, or of counting how many animals had been hunted and killed recently. Perhaps the bones were used as score-sheets for games like dice or jacks. If a messenger had to travel some distance to another tribe to ask them for something, or to deliver a complicated message, maybe he took a bone with him, marked in a certain way to remind him of the details of his message.

The invention of writing as we know it today

Writing as we understand it today was invented in the years between 3500 and 1500 BC, in at least seven different places. This is a very remarkable fact. At least seven different civilizations began to feel the need for a way of communicating which was more lasting and reliable than the human voice and memory, and all within 2000 years of each other. 2000 years is a very short time compared with how long people had been able to speak, and it's a tiny amount of time compared with how long men and women had been on the earth. It's quite probable that two or three of the civilizations heard at different times that one of the others had invented writing, but there was no copying. Each of the seven civilizations invented its own, individual system of writing.

The first people who are known to have invented writing were the Sumerians. The

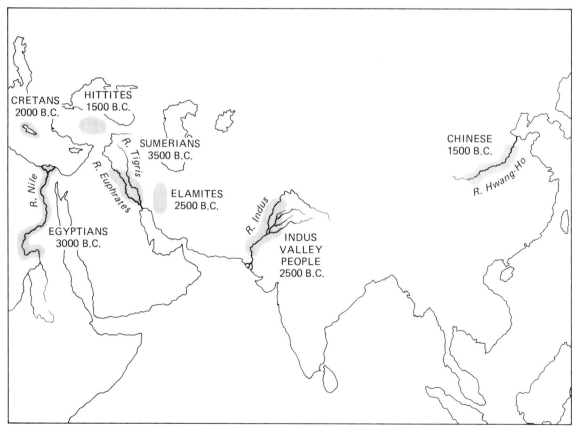

The first centres of writing

Sumerians lived in southern Mesopotamia, now part of Iraq, between 4000 and 3000 BC. Their system of writing developed towards the end of that time. About 3000 BC the Egyptians invented writing. They may well have got the idea from the Sumerians, but the two systems were quite different. About 500 years after that, the Elamites, a people living in an area now part of Iran, invented writing once again. Around the same time, 2500 BC, the civilization which lived in the valley of the river Indus, in modern Pakistan, invented writing for the fourth time. Another 500 years passed, and the people living on the Mediterranean island of Crete began writing. They probably got the idea from Egypt, but their system is definitely their own. Not only that, but the Cretans soon had two different kinds of writing. Whether this was because two different languages were spoken on the island, or because the Cretans wanted to write down the same language in two different ways, we don't know. Sometime before 1500 BC the Hittites, a people living in part of what is now Turkey, became the sixth inventors of writing. Last but not least, the Chinese invented writing at the same period, probably without any idea that something similar had been done in other parts of the world. The Chinese written in China today is directly related to the system invented there 3500 years ago.

Sorry about all these facts! Don't worry if you don't remember them first go; you can come back to them later, and the important thing is that you know where to find them if you need them.

Here's an activity which could become a major project if you want it to. Find out more about any of the seven civilizations we've mentioned in the last section. You'll probably need to use your school or college library, or go to a public library. It's likely that you'll find the most information on the Egyptians, the Sumerians and the Chinese.

Apart from encyclopaedias, these books are useful and interesting if you can find them:

Ancient China, by Richard L. Walker, published by Franklin Watts.
Cradle of Civilization, by S. N. Kramer, published by Time-Life Books.
Egypt the Black Land, by Paul Jordan, published by Phaidon.
The Egyptians, by Anne Millard, published by Macdonald.

From villages to cities

One question you might be asking is: why was writing invented in any case? If the human race had been going along for millions of years without it, why did they suddenly decide they needed it? The answer seems to be: cities. People were beginning to live in larger and larger communities. Once upon a time, the largest community had been the village. There might have been a string of villages, one every few miles along a river bank. Slowly, one of the villages became more important than the others. It became a town. The governor of that town was the most important figure in the area. Later on, the town grew into a city, and the city had a ruler, with a palace, a temple, priests, big markets, merchants who bought and sold goods from up and down the river.

In a village, everyone knows everyone else. Everyone knows which farmer owns which field and which animals. It's difficult to steal anything, unless you're going to run away from the village with it, because as soon as you show what you've stolen to anyone else, they're likely to know where it came from. In a city, everything is more complicated. In the ancient cities where writing was invented, the temple was very powerful, and owned a lot of land in the surrounding area. It was important for the priests of the temple to know exactly which land they owned, so they could work out how much rent to collect. It was important for merchants and businessmen, as the number of their customers increased, and as they traded further up and down the river, to have a way of remembering who had paid and who hadn't. Back in the simple days of the village past, human memory had been enough. Not any more.

But cities don't automatically produce writing. Only 450 years ago, the Spanish discovered, conquered and destroyed the magnificent civilization of the Incas in south America. The Incas were a people of great wealth and power, and skilful in many arts and crafts. Their civilization was based on cities, but they knew nothing about writing.

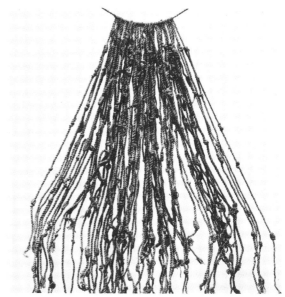

The Incas used a system of knots to keep all their business and government records

The ruined Inca city of Machu Picchu

1) If you enjoyed researching into the Egyptians or the Chinese, you should find the Incas equally interesting. Here are two books on the Inca civilization and the Spanish invasion:

> *The Incas* by C. A. Burland, published by Macdonald.
>
> *Peru under the Incas* by C. A. Burland, published by Evans Bros.

You decide how far to take this activity. You might just want to do some reading. Or you could make a page of notes as you read, to help your memory. Or you could do a full-scale piece of writing called *The Inca Civilization*, with illustrations, using the information you have collected.

2) Design your own developing community. Produce a series of (maybe three) drawings or maps, showing how a village became a town and then a city. As the community gets larger, there is a greater variety of buildings—markets, temples, banks, workshops, houses for the wealthy, houses for the poor. It doesn't matter how unlikely your designs are; be as imaginative as you want to.

Word pictures from Sumer, showing how they changed over time

Picture writing

All known systems of writing began with pictures. They all developed differently, because they were all serving different languages. They all started differently too, because people had different ideas about how to draw their pictures, and which pictures would mean which things. In this section are examples of some of the word-pictures of three of the peoples who invented writing; the Sumerians, the Egyptians and the Chinese.

The disadvantage of word-pictures is easy to find out if you try to do word-picture writing yourself. There are thousands of words in any language, so you need thousands of pictures to write them down. This means that writing is a difficult and slow business. In English, we

Word pictures from Egypt, showing how they changed over time

15

man	大	尺	人
hill	𝖶	凸	山
tree	𐊗	朮	木
dog	𓃡	𤝔	犬
moon	𓃾	𐊅	月
water	𓈗	𓈖	水
bird	𓅿	𐊾	鳥

Word pictures from China, showing how they changed over time

only have to learn 26 letters and we have the basic tools for writing. Imagine having to learn thousands of 'letters' at school, before you could be a proper writer. In ancient cities, only a very few people could write. They were called scribes. They had a long and hard training in school, which their parents had to pay for. If they passed the exam at the end, they would probably be scribes for life, writing letters, bills or accounts for priests, businessmen, or anyone who could afford the fee they charged for each piece of writing. Being a scribe was considered a very good job. About 2000 BC an Egyptian father sent his son off to writing school to learn to be a scribe. Here is part of what the father wrote to encourage his son to work hard:

'I have seen the metalworker at his work at the mouth of the furnace. His fingers were somewhat like crocodiles; he stank more than fish-roe...'

'The small building contractor carries mud....He is dirtier than vines or pigs from treading under his mud. His clothes are stiff with clay...'

'The arrow-maker, he is very miserable as he goes out into the desert (to get flint points). Greater is that which he gives to his donkey than its work thereafter (is worth)...'

'The laundry man launders on the (river) bank, a neighbour of the crocodile...'

'Behold, there is no profession free of a boss—except for the scribe: he is the boss...'

A model writing system

Here is a simple model of how a system of writing developed and changed. It's a model because the word-pictures and word-sounds we give are not actually Sumerian or Egyptian or Chinese. The word-pictures are made up by us and the word-sounds are those of English. But the model describes the kind of development and change which several of the ancient sytems went through.

A farmer owns some land. He wants to send a gift of some corn and a few grapes to a friend of his who has recently done him a favour. He decides to send his daughter with the gift. Being a bit of a show-off, he thinks he might get a note written for her to take to his friend. So he goes down to the local scribe in the town market-place and dictates a message. The scribe writes with the end of a sharp stick on a slab of damp clay about the size of a bar of chocolate. The note looks like this:

This means: 'I am sending my daughter from my house on a donkey to your house. She is bringing corn and grapes. What nice weather we're having.'

As you can see, each picture stands for at least one whole word. In fact, a picture often stands for more than one word. It stands for a whole idea.

The farmer pays the scribe for his work, takes the slab of clay home and leaves it to dry. The next day, off goes the daughter on the donkey, with corn, grapes and the letter.

16

Invent some word-pictures of your own. Try to write a few sentences, maybe telling a short story, using only pictures. Then write the story in English after the pictures. Or you could pass the pictures over to a friend without any words, and see how much your friend can understand of the story you are trying to tell. After that, you could try the process the other way round. Make up a simple story, or think of one you know already, maybe a traditional story, or a story from a television programme. Write the story down in English, and then translate it into pictures. If you do this in a group, you can all decide on the same story, do the pictures separately, and compare the results.

A way of getting word-pictures to do more work was to make each picture stand for several connected words. So, ☼ gradually came to mean not just *sun*, but *day* and *light* as well. In the farmer's message it meant *nice weather*. As well as *house*, ⌂ might be used for *home* and *family*. 🐴 might mean *ride* as well as *donkey*. ⇔ , a *mouth*, could also be used for *eat*.

This was a bit of an improvement, but not much. A big step forward came when scribes began to use the picture which meant a common word in the language every time the sound of that word was used in other words. That sounds complicated, so here's an example.

⇔ , we have agreed, first meant *mouth* and later *eat*. Now the sound of the word *eat* comes in many longer words, like *beat, seat, sheet, neat, meat, meet, treat, concrete, complete, street*. If the scribes could use ⇔ every time that sound came in the language, their job would be easier and they would be able to write down many more words than before.

Of course, there were still problems. How did they distinguish between *meet* and *meat* in their writing? Maybe like this:

👥⇔ = *meet*   🐂⇔ = *meat*

How did the scribes write down sounds where there were no small words to copy from, like the *b* in *beat*? Maybe a shape which stood for several short words beginning with *b*, like *buy*, *by* and *bye*, eventually came to be used just for the sound *b*.

Take six short, simple words. We'll give you six, and you can use them or others, as you like: *sea, ice, lay, oat, pie, ink.* Now make lists of longer words which include the sounds of the short words. So:

sea	*oat*
seat	note
seal	vote
ceiling	stoat.....

Notice that the spellings of the words don't matter here. We're only concerned about sounds. Now make up pictures for your short words. Next invent some sentences, and write them out in English. Here is one to start with:

Boats which are light capsize in gales.
Convert as much of each sentence as possible to pictures. Unless you're very clever, you won't be able to show every sound in the sentence as a picture. Our sentence might look like:

B🌾s 🧙 are ☼ ⛰⛰ 👀 in g🍺s.

If you like, choose sentences which go together to make a short story.

As the earliest writing systems developed, they used a mixture of word-pictures, shapes for parts of words, and shapes for individual sounds. The word-pictures changed over the centuries, until they didn't look anything like the thing they had first meant. You can see this by looking back at the tables on pages 15 and 16.

17

A love-letter picture

Opposite is a love-letter done in picture-writing by a girl of the Yukagir tribe in north-eastern Russia. It was written early in the 20th century. It is addressed to the girl's unfaithful ex-lover. It shows the girl (A) in skirt and pigtail (the dotted line near the skirt-top). She is alone in her house (B–C). The crossed bars (D) show that she feels deserted. Her ex-lover (E) lives to the left of her (F–G), with another girl. The writer of the letter knows that her ex-lover and his new girl are happy together (the squared-in crossed bars I). She expects that they will have two children (J and K). But she still feels very bitter that they are divided (L). She loves him, and her thoughts always go towards him (M), even though someone else (N) is in love with her.

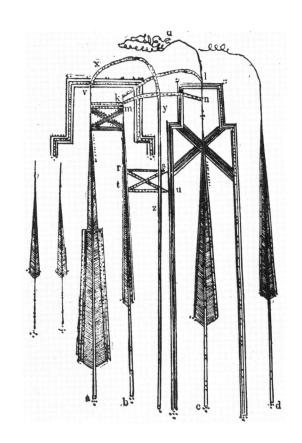

See if you can do a love-letter picture, a Valentine without words, which is as meaningful as the Yukagir girl's.

The alphabet

The route of the English alphabet

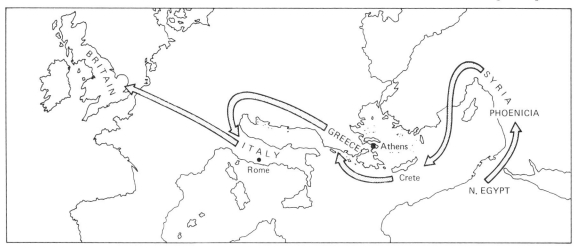

Both Sumerian and Egyptian writing developed into systems where almost all the shapes stood for parts of words, or syllables. Sumerian had about 100 shapes, or symbols; Egyptian had about 80. As we've already said, and everybody knows,

English has 26 symbols for its writing, and we call them *letters*. We've arranged the letters into an alphabet, and all the languages of western Europe use the same alphabet, with a few small variations. How did we come to do this?

18

Let's go backwards in time for a change. The English got their alphabet from Latin in the years after AD 600 (1400 years ago), when they were converted to Christianity. Latin was the language of the Romans for over a thousand years. So we owe our language to the Anglo-Saxons, and our system of writing to the Romans. The Romans got their alphabet from the Greeks. The Greeks got theirs from the Phoenicians about 900 BC. The Phoenicians were a people who lived on the east coast of the Mediterranean sea, the coast of what is now Israel, Syria and Lebanon. It seems to have been the Phoenicians who invented the alphabet. That is, they were the first people to invent a system of letters, where each letter stood for an individual sound in the language, instead of standing for a part of a word, or a whole word.

It's likely that the Phoenicians took a set of symbols from Egyptian, and used them as their letters. They didn't have any vowels in their writing; the Greeks put the vowels in later. Egyptian writing, as we have seen, was invented about 3000 BC. So the black shapes printed in front of you here have been through about 5000 years of development and change. Opposite you can see how this development probably happened with some of our modern English letters. Remember that although the Egyptian word-pictures originally meant the thing that they look like (the picture of an ox originally meant *ox*), by the time the Phoenicians got hold of them they stood for parts of words.

The great thing about an alphabet is that it's simple. 26 letters is much simpler than 100 syllable shapes or thousands of word-pictures. The simpler a system is, the more people will learn it. The more people learn to read and write, the more knowledge and ideas will be communicated. Of course, knowledge and ideas can be communicated for bad reasons as well as good, as we shall see later in the book. We can read and write, but that doesn't make us better than people who can't or couldn't. It may make us more complicated, but that's another thing.

Ancient Egyptian hieroglyphics	Sinai script	Moabite script	Early Phoenician	Western Greek	Early Greek	Modern English
∂	∂	K	K,∢	A,α	A	A
⬚ ⊏	⌒⊐	9	∫	B,B	B	B
YY	Ϥ	⌣	Y,Y	V,Y,Y	V	V
∿	∿	ⱳ	§ξ	M,M	M	M
⌇	⌐	y	↯	N,N	N	N
⬯	◊	o	o	O	o	O
⬭	Ƌ	◁	◁	D,R,P	R,R	R
	+	×†	+	T	T	T
⌣	w	w	w	ξSξ	ξS	S

1) We have said that being able to read and write doesn't make us better than people who can't or couldn't. Do you agree or disagree with this point of view?

2) Obviously being able to write is useful, but do you enjoy it? Do you avoid writing more than you have to? Make a list of the different occasions when you *have* to write, during the course of one week. What kind of writing do you do, and who do you do it for? Remember, we don't just mean writing in school or college. What kinds of writing do you actually enjoy, if any?

3) Look back over the second half of the chapter. How much have you learnt about the spread of languages and the development of writing? Anything? Some notes, or a summary of what you've read, could help to organize and fix the information in your mind.

2

Learning Our Own Language

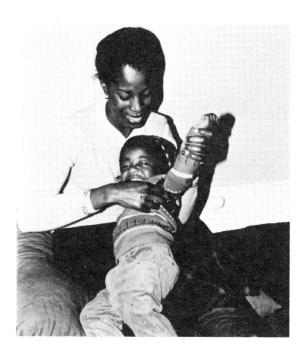

In the first chapter we mentioned some theories—ideas which people have put forward—about how language happened in the first place. We also said that nobody will ever know for certain how people began to talk. But two things are obvious; almost everybody in the world does talk, and almost everybody learns to talk by the time they are five years old. How do we do it? How do we learn our own language?

Believe it or not, people don't know the answer to that question either! And if someone thinks they've got the answer, there's always someone else around to disagree with it. Luckily, babies don't worry about how they learn language— they just get on and learn it.

To be fair, we must admit that people know much more about the question: *how do we learn our own language*? than about the question: *how did language happen in the first place*? There are millions of babies learning their own language around the world all the time. That means that there is plenty of evidence around for people to study.

A conversation

One of the writers of this book, Helen Savva, taped a conversation with a three-year-old boy called Joe. Here are some parts of it:

JOE:	Ouch!
HELEN:	Oh dear, did you bang your head?
JOE:	Yeh.
HELEN:	Does it hurt?
JOE:	Yeh.
HELEN:	Oh dear, shall I rub it?
JOE:	Yeh.

HELEN:	There we are then . . . is that better?
JOE:	Still hurts.
HELEN:	I'm sorry . . . there.
JOE:	Hurts.

****

JOE:	I've got a slide.
HELEN:	Where do you keep it?
JOE:	At Wally's.
HELEN:	(*Laughing*) You bought it where?
JOE:	I didn't bought it . . . I didn't get it.
HELEN:	Who got it then?
JOE:	Wally's had it.
HELEN:	Woolies?
JOE:	Yeh.
HELEN:	What's Woolies?
JOE:	A place where children go to.
HELEN:	A place where children go to ... right.
JOE:	Where does the sound go into?
HELEN:	On the tape-recorder?
JOE:	Mmm.
HELEN:	Er, the sound goes in through here, it's very small, isn't it?
JOE:	The . . . the sound goes in through that?
HELEN:	Yeh . . . goes in there and . . .
JOE:	Why . . . why does it go through that?
HELEN:	Why?
JOE:	Mmm.
HELEN:	Well, that's a microphone.
JOE:	Mmm.
HELEN:	Mmm, it's a very small microphone and it's very sensitive and it picks up our voices as we are talking, you see.
JOE:	Yeh.
HELEN:	And puts them onto . . .
JOE:	There.
HELEN:	The tape in there.
JOE:	Tape . . . mmm and what tape is it called that you've got it?
HELEN:	The tape . . . I'm not sure what the tape is called. We'll have a look when we take it out.
JOE:	Take it out and look.
HELEN:	In a minute.
JOE:	What time?
HELEN:	Well, in about five minutes. Hey, tell me where Suzy is.
JOE:	She's at the market.
HELEN:	Did you leave her at the market?
JOE:	Yeh.
HELEN:	What do you think she's going to buy there?
JOE:	A doughnut.
HELEN:	She just fancied going to the market, did she?
JOE:	She's going to buy a doughnut.
HELEN:	Oh, you've asked her to buy you a doughnut. Is that your favourite cake?
JOE:	(*Nods*)

****

HELEN:	Okay, what do you want to talk about?
JOE:	Ummm.
HELEN:	What would you like to tell me about?
JOE:	What I do.
HELEN:	Go on then, that's great. Tell me about what you do.
JOE:	I go to Tamlin's.
HELEN:	Good.
JOE:	(*Singing*) Tamlin . . .
HELEN:	Tell me what Tamlin looks like.
JOE:	Today he had a red jumper.
HELEN:	Yes . . . Is he blonde like you? Has he got blonde hair or dark hair?
JOE:	Er, he's got goldenish hair.
HELEN:	Goldenish?
JOE:	Yeh.
HELEN:	Like yours is it?
JOE:	Yeh, it's goldenish. Mine's goldenish.
HELEN:	Mmm, it's very nice.

JOE:	Yeh.
HELEN:	And what about the new baby Suzy's having?
JOE:	Might be blonde.
HELEN:	Might be blonde too, mightn't it? We don't know do we? Are you excited about it?
JOE:	Yes.

1) We would like to point out a few interesting things that we noticed in our transcript. (A transcript is a written-down version of something that was actually said.) Look back over the conversation, asking yourself questions about it, and studying certain parts in detail.

— Notice how Joe refuses to be fobbed off by Helen at the very beginning of the transcript when he insists that his head hurts.

— Notice the confusion between Helen and Joe about what and where Wally's is. Who is the more confused of the two? Joe has a clear idea that Wally's is *a place where children go to.* Helen thinks he might be talking about *Woolworth's*, the shop.

— Why do you think Joe changes the conversation so quickly when he and Helen have been talking about Wally's?

— Why does Joe say 'I didn't bought it' and then change to 'I didn't get it'?

— Think about Joe's sentence, 'Tape ... mmm and what is it called that you've got it?' Do you think there is more than one sentence in Joe's head at the same time?

— Why does Helen say 'Has he got *blonde hair* or *dark hair*?'? Would she say that when talking to an adult?

— Notice that Helen uses the word *blonde* but that Joe introduces a new word of his own, *goldenish*. When he talks about the baby that Suzy is expecting he says, 'Might be blonde.'

— Notice that Helen mishears Joe when he tells her that Suzy has gone to market to buy a doughnut. Helen thinks that Joe has said, 'Don't know.' But after

Helen's next question, Joe insists, 'She's going to buy a doughnut.' He says it very firmly.

— Are there times when Joe says things which an adult would not say?

— What is the longest sentence that Joe uses? About how long are most of his sentences (apart from *Yeh* and *Mmm*)?

— Would you know that this is a conversation between an adult and a young child, even if we hadn't told you? How?

— Your answers to some of these questions, and any other thoughts you have on the conversation, could become a piece of writing called *Joe and Helen Talking*.

2) It would be interesting and useful for you to have your own examples of young children talking. This isn't easy to organize, but it would be worth it if you could manage it. Tape children talking to you or to other children. If you don't have younger brothers or sisters, some of your friends probably have. It might even be possible to arrange a visit to a local primary school. Write down (or *transcribe*) what you think are the best parts of your tape.

Read your transcripts in groups. Perhaps you could take parts, and then talk about them together. Write down in note form what you find most interesting about the conversations. You may find that you have as many questions as answers. Some of the notes and questions about our transcript might be useful to you. If your conversation is between a young child and an older person, here are some more things to look out for:

— How many questions does the older person ask?

— How many questions does the child ask?

— Is the child very aware of the tape-recorder?

— Does the child ever change the subject?

— What tone of voice does the older person use?

— How long are the child's sentences?

— Does the child join sentences together or not?

— Does the child use any words or phrases which surprise you?

You may want to make up questions which suit your own transcript better. If your conversation is between two children, with no older person involved, there will be different questions to ask.

3) Both the activities above are difficult and demanding. Here are two more straight-forward activities:

a) Describe an incident, any incident, through the eyes of a young child. Try to use the language that the child might use, and see the incident as the child might see it.

b) Write a conversation between a child and an adult. If you like, set it out as a short play for two characters. It can be about anything you like.

Are babies blank or brilliant?

We've already said that there's a lot of disagreement about how we learn our language. Here are two of the theories which have been suggested to explain it. You must decide which one you prefer, or whether there is some truth in both of them, or whether there are important things which both have missed out.

The Blank Baby Theory

When the human baby is born, it knows nothing at all; its mind is blank. The baby begins to learn language by hearing the language used by its parents, its brothers and sisters, or anyone else who happens to be looking after it. Parents are usually delighted when their baby makes its first sounds and respond by rewarding the baby with affection and by talking back to the baby. The baby continues to make sounds and later words and then groups of words, until its language is like the language that adults use. This theory suggests that babies learn language by

copying the sounds that adults make until they get them right, and hearing so many words and sentences spoken that they gradually build up their own collection. When the collection gets to a certain size, you can say that the child has learnt the language.

The Brilliant Baby Theory

Human babies are born already fixed up to learn language. They have equipment on board which no baby animal has. That equipment makes them good at learning language very fast. After all, language is very, very complicated. It's not just a case of learning to copy sounds. There are very detailed rules about how words are put together to make sense. Learning our own language may be the most difficult piece of brainwork we do all our lives. How could babies do it so successfully and

quickly if they were born blank? They must have a mini-computer in their heads which can take sounds that adults make, understand the language rules behind those sounds, and then use those rules to say phrases or sentences which they have never actually heard adults say.

We are not going to say which of these two theories is right. There are things to be said for both of them. Think carefully about each of them, and try to decide which are the strong and weak points in the two arguments.

Here is a conversation between a mother and a child:

CHILD: My teacher holded the rabbits and we patted them.
MOTHER: Did you say your teacher held the rabbits?
CHILD: Yes.
MOTHER: What did you say she did?
CHILD: She holded the baby rabbits and we patted them.
MOTHER: Did you say he held them tightly?
CHILD: No, she holded them loosely.

Now, the interesting thing here is why the child says *holded* and not *held*. Can you suggest a reason for this? The child hasn't learnt to say *holded* by copying adult speech because adults don't say *holded*, they say *held*. The child ignores the mother's attempt to correct *holded* to *held* and continues to say it her own way. It seems very likely that she has learnt that *-ed* is a very common ending to put on verbs when they are done and finished with—when something has happened in the past. *I start tomorrow*, but *I started yesterday. You like oranges*, but *You liked that film we saw last week.* But there are some verbs that tell us they're in the past in other ways. *She sees him often*, but *She saw him two hours ago. My teacher holds the rabbits*, but *My teacher held the rabbits.* The child has learnt a rule about *-ed* endings, but she hasn't yet learnt the exceptions to that rule. Even though she has made a mistake, it's a clever mistake to make.

Have you ever heard a child say *mines* instead of *mine*? Here is Katie talking with Peter about some pieces of a building game which she thinks are hers:

KATIE: Don't crush mines up!
PETER: What was yours? What was it?
KATIE: Dis is mines.
PETER: That's yours, okay.

Think about Katie's use of the word *mines*. Katie has learnt that many similar words end in *s*. *Its, his, hers, ours, theirs,* and *yours* all end in *s*. So, Katie might say, *that's hers* or *it's his* and it makes perfect sense to Katie to say *Dis is mines*.

Later on, the children will learn to say *This is mine* and *My teacher held the rabbits.* The kinds of 'mistakes' which adults often laugh at, can show that young children are trying out important rules about language. Like all of us, they need to make mistakes to learn.

Try to remember 'mistakes' which you made as a young child learning to speak. Perhaps your parents sometimes remind you of them. Maybe you've heard other young children doing similar things. If you can think of several examples, put them together in a piece of writing called *Young Children Talking* or *Things Children Say.*

Baby talk

On the whole, we don't talk to young children in the same way that we talk to someone of our own age. Most of us make an effort to make our sentences simple. Some adults use their own version of baby talk. Sometimes, older people don't particularly help babies by the way they speak to them. Here is an extract from a book called *Ulysses* by James Joyce, in which a girl named Cissy uses baby language when talking to a very young baby:

— Say papa, baby. Say pa pa pa pa pa pa pa.

And baby did his level best to say it for he was very intelligent for eleven months everyone said and big for his age and the picture of health, a perfect bunch of love, and he would certainly turn out to be something great, they said.

— Haja ja ja haja.

Cissy wiped his little mouth with the dribbling bib and wanted him to sit up properly, and say pa pa pa but when she undid the strap she cried out, holy saint Denis, that he was possing wet and to double the half blanket the other way under him. Of course his infant majesty was most obstreperous at such toilet formalities and he let everyone know it:

— Habaa baaaahabaaa baaaa.

And two great big lovely big tears coursing down his cheeks. It was no use soothering him with no, nono, baby, no and telling him about the geegee and where was the puffpuff but Ciss, always readywitted gave him in his mouth the teat of the suckingbottle and the young heathen was quickly appeased.

Young children can completely misunderstand a word or phrase which an adult uses to them, as Laurie Lee, the author of *Cider with Rosie*, did on his first day at school:

I spent that first day picking holes in paper, then went home in a smouldering temper.

'What's the matter, Love? Didn't he like it at school, then?'

'They never gave me the present.'

'Present? What present?'

'They said they'd give me a present.'

'Well, now, I'm sure they didn't.'

'They did! They said: "You're Laurie Lee, aren't you? Well just you sit there for the present." I sat there all day but I never got it. I ain't going back there again.'

Here's a list of questions for you to talk about in a group:
1) Do you like talking to young children?
2) How do you talk to them? What tone of voice do you use?
3) Do you ever have difficulty in understanding young children?
4) Do young children ever have difficulty in understanding you?
5) If the answer to 3 or 4 is *Yes*, can you explain why?

The first five years

Between the age of 0, when a newborn baby says no words at all, and the age of 5, when a child has a nearly complete language, much learning happens. Every baby is different, and the exact times and kinds of learning vary. But it is possible to point out roughly the stages which normal babies go through in learning their language.

At the age of three or four months, babies begin to make a series of sounds, but these sounds are not words. They are cooing and babbling noises which are

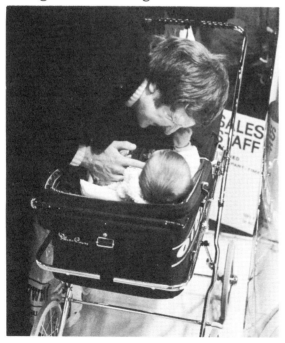

something like speech, but we cannot understand these noises.

Between six and nine months the noises become a bit more organized. There is rhythm in the sounds a baby makes and a tone of voice begins to emerge. Parents may feel that the baby is trying to tell them something or the baby may make a similar sound whenever it wants mummy, daddy or a favourite toy.

At about a year children begin to say their first words. Some children stop babbling, but others continue to produce long babbled sentences while they learn new words. There is a close link between babbling and the first words a child speaks. But there is a definite step forward from sounds which we cannot understand to words which we do understand, because in order to produce words the child has to make the correct sequence of sounds.

Children make words easier for themselves. They might say *mama* for *mother*, *dada* for *daddy*, *ba* for *baby* or *da* for *dog*. When a child has learned about 50 words it begins to make sounds in a regular way. At this stage, it might leave off the first sounds of many words, saying *ilk* for *milk*, *mack* for *smack*, or *ally* for *Sally*.

Children at this age find certain sounds easier than others, depending on where they appear in a word. At the beginning of a word children find it easier to say *d, b* and *g* than *t, p* and *k*. So a child might say *botty* for *potty* or *dea* for *tea*. The changes that a child makes are not just a matter of chance; they do form a pattern.

Children begin to communicate by saying single words. But in order to communicate more complex meaning, children have to learn how to put words together in sequence so that they make sense. The child has to learn the grammar of language, the rules that tell us how words can be joined together to make sentences. At about 18 months children begin to join words together: *dada gone, my car, mummy hat, teddy bed, my chair.*

You can see that even at this early age children are putting words together in a particular way. They are sensitive to the ways in which adults join words together. It is remarkable, when you consider all the possible ways in which children could order their words, that they choose a way which makes sense. A child is more likely to say *me fall* than *fall me*, or *milk gone* than *gone milk*.

Later, the child goes on to put three or four words together: *mummy read me, my dolly hurt, look my teddy, Lisa kick the ball.* Children learn to ask questions, first by just making their voices rise at the end of a phrase—*I have some?*—and then using words like *why, where* and *when: where we can go?* They learn to use negatives, first by simply adding *not* to a phrase: *this mine, this not mine.* Later on, more complicated ways of saying *not* appear, like *I can't come.*

The two years between 18 months and 3½ are very important. Most of the basic rules of a language are learnt by then. Of course, they're not learnt as rules; they're learnt as experience. No sensible adult sits down with a three-year-old child and says, 'Today we're going to learn the rules for asking questions'. If anyone were foolish enough to do that, they would certainly do more harm than good.

By the age of 3½, the child has probably learnt that a sentence can be made longer by adding on another part with *and:*

Paul gone in garden and he playing.

But short sentences, one after the other, are still the most common:

I don't want my hat. Take off.

I finished. I want to get down.

The next step for the child is to understand that sentences don't just exist in isolation, by themselves. One sentence relates to another sentence. Also, words aren't necessarily fixed. Their meaning can change depending on the object they are describing. *Big* means something different in *big bus* from what it means in *big spoonful. A thick jumper* and a *thick fog* make *thick* mean different things.

At the age of 3, most children can handle *big* and *little* if they are describing something that they know well, like a toy or a piece of clothing. If children are given an object they don't know very well and asked whether it is big or little, they may get very confused, and try to use their own size to compare the object to. Words like *thick/thin* and *wide/narrow* are more difficult. Other words which are not fixed and which the child must learn are *here/there, my/your* and *this/that:*

Shall we stay in here or go out there?

Would you like to go into this shop or that shop?

These are just a few of the many tasks which a child's brain has to cope with. Amazingly, almost all children are successful. They do it, and they do it without being taught. By the age of 5 they have done the most complicated job of learning that they may ever do.

Unusual experiences

However, there are some children who don't learn language normally, or don't learn it at all. Some children have brains which are physically damaged. Blind, deaf and dumb children have to face particular difficulties. Some children have very unusual experiences; we talked about Victor, the wild boy of Aveyron, in Chapter 1. Let's look at some other cases of children who, for one reason or another, have not made the progress which normal children make.

Think about the problems facing a young child whose parents are both deaf.

Jim could hear perfectly normally, but both his parents were very deaf. They communicated to each other by using sign language, and they only had a few words of speech. Jim's parents didn't try to teach him sign language and he didn't have very much contact with other children. He did, however, watch a great deal of television, and he learned a few words from this.

When Jim was 3 years and 9 months old,

he was discovered by speech therapists (people who help children and adults who have difficulty in speaking). Jim knew and understood far less than most children of his age. The sounds he made were unusual and therefore he couldn't communicate successfully. He tried to talk to other people, but his words did not go together in the order which made sense. Here are some examples of Jim's speech at 3 years and 9 months:

That enough two wing.
Fall that back.
Going house a fire truck.
Be down go.

Jim had decided for himself how to put words together in sequence, because he didn't hear normal speech. Fortunately, Jim received regular help and quickly caught up with other children of his own age. He also learnt sign language so that he could communicate with his parents.

Grace and Virginia are identical twins who live in California. When they were about 17 months old, they began to make up their own private language. One of the girls would pick something up and name it, and her sister would agree. For the next five years the twins spoke only in their own language. In the girls' language, Virginia's name is Cabenga and Grace's name is Poto. Grace might say, 'Snap aduk Cabenga, chas die-dipana', and at once both girls would play with their doll's house.

When the twins were born, their grandmother arrived from Germany to look after them, as both their parents had to go out to work. Grandmother spoke only German. The girls' American father spoke English, and their German-born mother spoke a mixture of German and English. The twins had little contact with other children because their grandmother was very protective towards them and they lived more or less in a private world. However, they did live in an area with a large Spanish community, so that they probably heard Spanish spoken too. They could understand their father's English,

Grace and Virginia—Poto and Cabenga

their grandmother's German and their mother's German/English mixture. With all the different languages spoken around them, the twins invented one of their own. No one else could understand it.

At first people thought that the twins were backward. They were sent to a school for the mentally handicapped. However, they learnt sign language so quickly that they obviously were not backward. So psychologists kept moving them from one special school to another. Eventually, the twins found themselves in a clinic run by a Dr Hagen. Here they talked and played, closely watched by psychologists and linguists. At the same time, they were taught to speak English. One of the main problems in understanding what they were saying was that they talked very fast indeed, much faster than the normal speed of English:

'Cabenga, padem manibadu peeta,' says Grace.

'Doan nee bada tengkmatt, Poto,' answers Virginia.

For a while the twins became famous. People wrote about them and their family in magazines; films were made about them. Now that the twins have learnt to speak English and go to an ordinary school, interest in them is dying down and they are having to adjust to being ordinary children. Perhaps, in some ways, that's the best thing that could happen.

Dr Hagen believes that the girls really did invent a language of their own, complete with nouns, verbs and a grammatical framework. However, their language does have English, German and Spanish words in it, as well as words that they invented themselves.

The stories of the twins and of Jim have more or less happy endings. But there are other stories of young children who for one reason or another have been locked away and deprived of human company for long periods of time. These stories often don't end happily. Two parents in Los Angeles locked their daughter Genie away for almost 14 years because her father believed that she was mentally retarded, which she was not. When Genie was discovered, she was disturbed emotionally. She had normal hearing and vision but could only understand a few words. She had been given enough food to keep her alive, but no one ever spoke a kind word to her. For much of the time she was kept tied to a chair.

Genie is an adult now and lives in a foster-home. She has learnt English as a result of hearing other people around her use the language. However, after several years, Genie still has problems sounding her words. Her use of language is limited.

Children learn their own language as long as they are surrounded by people who speak that language. If children don't have a normal experience of language, as Jim, Genie and the twins didn't (though for very different reasons), they don't learn their own language like most children do.

---

1) Write in any form you choose about Grace and Virginia. You might be a journalist writing an article on the twins. Or you might write a conversation between the twins' parents expressing concern about the girls' mysterious language. You could even imagine that you are Dr Hagen, studying a private language which you don't understand, trying to work out what it means.

2) Look back over the three stories we've just described. What were the crucial experiences which caused Jim, Genie and the twins to develop in the way they did?
3) Write a story, a play or a conversation about a child or young person whose experience of language has been very unusual.

In this chapter, we have talked about *our own language* as if we all know exactly what we mean. For most of you reading this, your own language is English. For some of you, your own language is Greek, or Spanish, or Urdu, or Bengali, and you have learnt English as well. In Chapters 3 and 4, we hope to see that deciding what *our own language* is, can be more complicated—and more interesting—than you might think.

3
English Languages

One of the most important things to understand about language is that it's always changing. It's changing in time. The English spoken 400 years ago is different from the English spoken today, which is different from the English that will be spoken in 400 years' time. The same is true of every language in the world. Languages change as time goes by.

Languages change in time, and they change in space as well. That means that the English spoken by most people in one part of the world (say London) is different from the English spoken by most people in Edinburgh, New York, Sydney, or the country parts of west Yorkshire. The French spoken in Paris is different from the French spoken by most people in the south of France, or on the island of Martinique in the West Indies.

Thirdly, languages change according to who you are. A bank manager speaks differently from a greengrocer. The prime minister speaks differently from a tea-lady

in the Houses of Parliament, even though they live and work in the same city. But *who you are* doesn't mean quite the same thing as *how rich you are*. A millionaire might have made his money out of selling scrap metal, and might have hung on to the way he spoke when he was poor. Henry Cooper, the ex-boxer, a very rich man indeed, has kept most of his Cockney way of speaking.

In the next two chapters of the book we're going to look at a wide variety of differences within one language—English. However, a lot of what we say about differences in English is true of differences in many other languages as well, and those other languages are just as interesting and just as important as English.

Differences are good

The first thing to be said about the different ways in which people have used and are using English is: differences are good. Variety in language is an excellent thing. Imagine that the same kind of English were spoken all over over the world. Imagine that the same kind of English had been spoken all over the world for the last 500 years. You would have something which was very, very boring. The same song sung over and over again. No new words, no new ideas, no new ways of saying things. In fact, people would probably have got so bored with English that they would have stopped using it. The language would be dead.

But then, here is an extract from a novel by Bill Naughton called *One Small Boy*. The small boy is Irish, his name is Michael M'Cloud, and he goes to school in Bolton, Lancashire. The story is set about 60 years ago.

After three o'clock playtime on the Wednesday, Miss Skegham began poetry lesson. The class was divided into four seasons, and each one had to chant a verse suitable to the season.

'Sheed, let me hear you give Spring,' said Miss Skegham. 'The rest of the class silence.'

Sheed faced her, giving a whisper first, 'I'll spring you . . . ,' and then opening the right side of his mouth: '"Summer is a-comin' in,"' he piped, '"loudly sing cackoo."'

'Cuckoo,' she corrected.

'Cookoo, Cookoo,' he trilled.

He admired the boy's coolness. If she asks me, he thought, I'll drop dead. 'M'Cloud,' she called, 'let's hear "The North Wind" from you.'

He stood facing her and the circle of faces, his heart shaking, and praying mentally for help from the Virgin, he forced his dry voice out:

> ' "The North Wind doth blow,
>   And we shall have snow,
>   "And what will the robin do then, poor ting?
>   He'll . . . . . " '

'*Ting*?' she repeated. 'Poor *ting*? say "thing". Start from the beginning again. No need for you others to titter.'

Ting, thing, ting, thing? He cleared his throat but couldn't remember the opening. She said: ' "The North wind doth blow . . . " ' He coughed. The blood felt up to his eyes. Ting? thing? He'd have to watch for that. 'Right,' she said. He began: ' "The North wind doth blow. And we shall have snow, And what . . . " '. 'Not so fast,' she said. 'Go on. "And what . . . " '. ' "And what, and what will the robin do then . . . " ' it was somewhere near and he'd have to watch out for it, they were all listening and watching him. 'Go on,' she said. He went on: ' "And what, what will the robin do then, poor t'ting . . . " '

'Ting! ting!' she said and he heard them all snigger. 'Don't you know the king's English yet, M'Cloud?'

King's English—I'm Irish. She's saying that against the Irish. The flush died down and his face went cool. '*Thing*!' she called out, '*thing, thing, thing*. Class, say "poor thing".' They let out one loud, 'Poor thing.' 'Right, M'Cloud,' she said, in a rather kindly voice: 'Yes, "The North Wind . . . " ' The nice touch in her voice almost started him, but not quite. 'M'Cloud,' she shouted, 'come on, "The North Wind . . . " '

He stood unbudging. He saw her eyes bulge and the redness swarm up her throat as she came up to him and gave him a swinging slap on the side of the head. It made things spin for a moment, but he didn't feel any pain, and he stood as erect as he could, feeling that half the side of his face was missing: 'Now will you say it?' she asked. He didn't speak. He could only half see her, for the spots were still jumping. 'Right,' she said, going for her cane. 'Hold out your hand.' He put his right hand out and she held up the cane. It came down clean across the palm. 'The other,' she said. He held the left hand out. The cane came down with a sharper rush. It made him tremble with pain. She waited a second: 'Now,' she said, 'we'll have "The North Wind doth blow." '

He stood there trying to stop all his body from shaking. The pain was simple to bear, but he longed for a calm moment to come to him. He didn't speak. She thrust her cane under his right armpit and nudged his arm out. She gave him a rap on it. Then she gave him a rap on the other hand. He hoped the tears wouldn't start. He found running through his mind the words, 'Brave Robert Emmet, the darling of Erin, Brave Robert Emmet he died with a smile,' in answer to the king's English. The class had gone very silent. She said: 'Right, M'Cloud. Now we'll have "The North Wind doth blow . . . " ' He felt the turn of heart inside him, and something in his mind said, you won't! It was alright now, that calm thing had come, and she could crucify him and he wouldn't cry, nor would he ever say 'The North Wind'.

He felt himself caught by the ear, and pulled up to the front of the class, just below her desk where she forced him down on his knees: 'Kneel there,' she said, 'and kneel up straight. Keep your hands behind your back. And tell me when you're ready to say "The North Wind ... "'. I'll stay here happily, he thought, till there's a hole in the ground.

We have a problem here. We said just now that differences in language are good. The teacher in the story doesn't think so. She thinks that the boy is being lazy, or stupid, or deliberately rude when he says: '"And what will the robin do then, poor ting?"' There are plenty of people around who would agree with her. These days, not many people (not even teachers!) would actually hit children for speaking in a particular way—unless they were really being deliberately rude, which is a different matter. But many people still believe that some ways of speaking *are* lazy, or stupid, or ignorant.

Most people, sometime in their lives, have been laughed at, sneered at, teased, criticized or corrected for the way they speak. The teasing might have been gentle and friendly; the sneering might have been vicious. 'Posh' ways of speaking are criticized as much as 'rough' ways of speaking. If this has ever happened to you, try to write about it. If it hasn't, you're lucky. If it's happened to someone you know, write about that. If it's never happened to you or to anyone you know, make up a story about someone who is laughed at or criticized for the way they speak. The someone could be: a foreign person coming to live in Britain for the first time; a tourist going on holiday abroad; a pupil in a school who speaks differently from most of the other kids.

Accent and dialect

At this point we're going to introduce two words which will make it easier for us to talk about different kinds of language. The two words are *accent* and *dialect*.

Accent means *the way people pronounce words*. Everybody has an accent. In all languages with more than a few thousand speakers, you can find different accents within the same language. In fact, the same person might completely change his or her accent during a lifetime, or even move from one accent to another within five minutes. Imagine someone on the phone talking to his boss, and then having to shout out of the window to the dustman. There might well be a difference in the actual sounds he uses to say the same word to the two different people. The newsreader on the BBC has just as much of an accent as, say, a bus driver in Newcastle. If the newsreader says that the bus driver has a strong Newcastle accent, that's because the sounds the bus driver uses to make some of his words are quite different from the sounds the newsreader uses. As far as the bus driver's concerned, the newsreader has a strong accent as well.

Dialects are different forms of the same language. The main differences between dialects are in some of the actual words used by a speaker, or in the way the words are arranged in sentences. When we talked at the beginning of the chapter about the different kinds of English spoken in different parts of the world, and about the differences in language depending on who you are, we were talking about dialects. As with accents, everybody has a dialect.

It's easy to muddle up *accent* and *dialect*, and a lot of people do. They might say: 'So-and-so's got a funny accent', and think that's the only thing to be said about so-and-so's language. Probably they do that because the sound someone makes when speaking is the most obvious thing about their language; it's what you notice first, and a person's accent is carried in the sounds they make.

---

1) Compare different accents. It's quite likely that there are people in your class or group who have different accents. You'll need a tape-recorder. Take a short piece of writing—a poem, or a piece from the newspaper—and get several people to read it onto the tape. Listen to the readings, and try to decide if there are differences between the accents of any of the readers. If everybody in your class speaks the same way, you'll need to include a teacher, or someone from another class who you know has a different accent. Be careful how you ask people. Be friendly. People are sensitive about their language!

2) You might find the last activity too difficult, too frightening, or perhaps you just haven't got a tape-recorder. Here's an activity you can do by yourself with only pen and paper. Take a short piece of writing, yours or someone else's. Write it out on alternate lines of a piece of paper. Now say it to yourself aloud, and as you do so, write it out underneath your first version exactly as you say it. Here's an example:

One of the main problems with the English language is the spelling
Wun ov the mayeen problemz with the inglish langwidj iz the spehling
system. Many people find it hard to remember how to spell words.
system. Mehnee peepel faaeend it haad too remehmbur haoo too spel wurdz.
This is not their fault. English spellings are very illogical.
This iz not thair forlt. Inglish spehlingz aar vehree ilojikel.

You will definitely come across some difficulties when you're doing this. There will be some sounds which you won't know how to write down exactly as they're said. You'll have to decide what to do. You might even invent new letters for certain sounds.

One thing should be clear. Nobody writes the way they speak. English writing is very peculiar.

---

1) Take the five English vowels: *a, e, i, o, u.* Make lists of words, one list for each vowel, showing the different sounds the vowel can make, without the help of another vowel, in different words. So:

a
cat
gate
stare   etc.

When you've done all the vowels by themselves, try the same thing with combinations of two vowels together, like *ea, ei, ai, eu.* So:

ei
their
conceit
either   etc.

2) Write down as many examples as you can remember, of 'silent' letters—letters which go into a word when you write it, but not when you say it. Start with: lam*b*, thou*gh*t, whis*t*le.

A while ago we were talking about accent and dialect, and now we've had three activities in a row to do with writing and spelling. Why? To point out that whatever accent or dialect you have, talking and writing are two different things, though closely connected. Nobody's accent or dialect automatically makes writing easier, or harder, for them.

'Here is the nine o'clock news'

Let's look at some different dialects. Here is one that most people hear every day, whether they use it themselves or not:

Good evening. Here is the nine o'clock news. The September unemployment figures show an increase of 150,000 over the figures for August, and a rise of nearly a quarter of a million over the equivalent figures for September of last year. A spokesman for the Department of Employment said this afternoon that the bulk of the increase has been caused by the large number of school leavers who are still unable to find work.

The prime minister, Mrs Thatcher, today flew to Washington for talks with President Reagan. It is expected that their discussions will centre on the need, which both countries now face, to limit energy consumption . . .

It may surprise you to see the nine o'clock news used as an example of dialect. You may say: 'That's not a dialect. That's ordinary English'. In fact, there's no such thing as 'ordinary English'. The English of the nine o'clock news, of most television and radio programmes, of the newspapers, the English which school books are written in, is a dialect of English like any other (or rather, not like any other). It's a very important dialect, because business, government and communications media all use it. It's the dialect which people nearly always use when they write. Here we are using it now. It's a valuable dialect to be able to control, to use when you need it. But it's not better, or nicer sounding, or cleverer, or more complicated, than any other dialect. All dialects are equally good.

The dialect of the nine o'clock news is called Standard English—SE for short. That's a misleading name for a start, because *Standard* means something suspiciously like *correct*, as if SE were saying: 'I'm right, and all the others are wrong'. Many people whose dialect is SE—that is, they use it all day themselves, as well as hearing it on the nine o'clock news—do have a nasty habit of saying exactly that. 'The way I speak is correct, and other ways of speaking are incorrect.' The reason they do this is not that they're nasty people. They may be very nice people. The reason why many people believe that there is such a thing as *correct English* is that some of the most powerful people who speak English, at various times in the history of the language, decided to call their dialect *correct*. And most other people believed them.

The nine o'clock news is a good way of showing the difference between accent and dialect. If you live in Wales or Scotland or Ireland, and you hear the news read in English, the newsreader's dialect is SE, with maybe one or two very small differences from the London newsreader's dialect. But the newsreader's accent is Welsh or Scottish or Irish. This is because SE is not a *regional* dialect. It doesn't depend on where you live. It's a 'who you are' dialect. So we'll call it a *social class* dialect. You can speak SE with a Scottish, or Yorkshire, or Somerset, or Jamaican, or Australian accent.

We have said that all dialects are equally good, that everyone has a dialect, everyone has an accent. We have also said that SE, although an important dialect, is not better than any other. Do you agree or disagree with these statements? Discuss them in a group. Remember, you don't have to agree with what we've said just because it's written in a book.

One conversation—three dialects

Three girls are talking. Two of them are called Angela, the other is called Shirley. They can speak three dialects each. Like most people who live in London, they speak Cockney. Because their parents came to England from Jamaica, they speak Jamaican. And because they go to school, listen to the teachers, read books and hear the nine o'clock news, they speak SE. They decide to have the same short

conversation in the three dialects. There was a tape-recorder running on the table, and we have written down what they said. They give their Jamaican way of speaking the proper name, which is *Jamaican creole*.

SHIRLEY: Now Angela I want you and the other Angela to have a conversation in, um, the Jamaican creole, not very long, just for a little while, and then repeat it in English afterwards if you can.

ANGELA 1: Wha' happen Angie? How's things getting on at school, cool?

ANGELA 2: Yeh, they cool, y'know.

ANGELA 1: How's you mother?

ANGELA 2: She alright.

ANGELA 1: Me see you brother a' home downa Brixton Market de other day y'know, inna record shop.

ANGELA 2: Me know what him a do down dere 'cause if me mumma catch him she wring him neck fi him y'know.

SHIRLEY: Okay. Thank you. Now could . . . .

ANGELA 1: Alright Angie, later, right?

ANGELA 2: Yeh, later.

SHIRLEY: Yeh. Could you er . . . repeat that in English please? Find some way to . . .

ANGELA 2: Right, well she said to me, "Hello . . ."

SHIRLEY: No, I mean I want you to say it, like a conversation a bit like before.

ANGELA 2: Hello, Angie!

ANGELA 1: Alright Angie, how are you?

ANGELA 2: Fine thank you.

ANGELA 1: I saw your brother in Brixton Market the other day in a record shop.

ANGELA 2: I don't know what he's doing down there, 'cause if my mother catches him she'll wring his neck for him.

ANGELA 1: Okay then, I'll see you later, okay?

ANGELA 2: Yeh, see you.

ANGELA 1: Bye.

ANGELA 2: Bye.

SHIRLEY: There we have two different types of dialect, one in Jamaican creole, and one in English.

ANGELA 1: (*whispering*) Cockney now, Cockney.

SHIRLEY: Um, there's another sort of a dialect, called Cockney, and I wonder if you could repeat that little scene again.

ANGELA 1: Watcher Ang!

ANGELA 2: Watcher.

ANGELA 1: 'Ow yer gettin' on at school?

ANGELA 2: Alright.

ANGELA 1: 'Ow's yer mum?

ANGELA 2: She's alright.

ANGELA 1: I saw your brother in Brixton the other day . . .

ANGELA 2: Did yer?

ANGELA 1: . . . I seen him round there, yeh, he was in this record shop.

ANGELA 2: I dunno what 'e's doing there 'cause if my mum catches 'im she'll wring 'is neck for 'im you know.

ANGELA 1: Oh yeh?

ANGELA 2: Yeh.

ANGELA 1: Alright Ang, I'll see yer, right?

ANGELA 2: Yeh, see yer.

ANGELA 1: Bye.

ANGELA 2: Yeh, bye.

ANGELA 1: Give me regards to yer mum, won't yer?

ANGELA 2: Yeh, same to you love.

SHIRLEY: Right, there . . . (laughing) . . there we have three different dialects.

When you write down what people have actually said, you lose one important part of their language—the sound, the accent. So we've tried to make up for that a bit, by spelling some of the words as they were said, rather than as they're usually spelt.

---

1) Look at three conversations again, and write down all the differences which you can see between the three dialects.

2) Do the same thing as the three girls have done. Have a conversation, or make up a short drama scene, and perform it in more than one dialect. Perhaps you don't normally use more than one dialect yourself; if you don't, then try to get into a dialect you know of. You don't have to use three dialects. You could just use SE and your local regional dialect, whatever that is. You can do this activity in pairs or small groups. Or, if you want to write the conversations straight down instead of performing them, you can work by yourself. We think you'll get better results, however, if you try the language aloud before writing it down.

3) Make up your own nine o'clock news, or News at Ten, or weather forecast, and 'translate' it into a local dialect.

When people want to write in a dialect which is not SE, they often spell words differently from the usual way, to try to show how the words are said in the dialect. (We did this just now with the Jamaican and the Cockney conversations.) In some ways this is not a very logical thing to do, because there are many, many words in SE which are said and written differently, like *thought, doubt, write, work, great*. It is a mistake to believe that SE is very similar to normal writing and spelling, and that all other dialects are very different from normal writing and spelling.

What is 'posh'?

While we're on the differences between writing and talking, and between dialect and accent, we'll introduce you to one more phrase which you might find useful. We've said that many people speak SE using a local accent. This is true. But it's also true that some people use a special accent which is sometimes referred to as 'talking posh'—the London nine o'clock newsreader, for example. The proper name for this 'posh' accent is *received pronunciation*, RP for short. RP and SE are *not* the same thing, because there are more people who speak the SE dialect than people who use the RP accent. RP is a social class accent, so that you find RP speakers all over Britain, Ireland and many other parts of the world where English is spoken.

Writing in dialect

Dialect writing normally comes in plays, in stories (especially when people are talking to each other), or in poetry. If someone is applying for a job in a bank, describing a chemistry experiment or filling in a tax form, it would be sensible to use SE, because SE is the accepted dialect for those kinds of writing. But, in theory, other dialects would do just as well; there is nothing inadequate about them, nothing which makes them incapable of doing the job. It is a question of what people have come to expect and accept. SE, of course, is not *just* for tax forms and chemistry experiments. Many, many people have used SE for stories, novels, plays and poetry, as well.

Here are some pieces of writing which use different English dialects. The first is from Barry Hines' famous book *A Kestrel for a Knave*, which is set in Barnsley, Yorkshire. Billy, the main character, is talking to his older brother, Jud. They are downstairs in the house, very early in the morning. Jud is just off to work, down the mine. Notice that Barry Hines has written the dialogue—the parts where Billy and Jud are actually talking to each other—in the local dialect, and the narrative—the parts where the writer himself is describing what is happening—in SE.

'It's a smashing morning again.'

'Tha wouldn't be saying that if tha wa' goin' where I'm goin'.'

Jud poured himself another cup of tea. Billy watched the last dribbles leaving the spout, then put a match to the gas. The kettle began to rumble immediately.

'Just think, when we're goin' up t'woods, tha'll be goin' down in t'cage.'

'Ar, just think; an' next year tha'll be coming down wi' me.'

'I'll not.'

'Won't tha?'

'No, 'cos I'm not goin' to work down t'pit.'

'Where are tha goin' to work, then?'

Billy poured the boiling water on the stained leaves in the pot.

'I don't know; but I'm not goin' to work down t'pit.'

'No, and have I to tell thi why? . . . '

He walked into the kitchen and came back carrying his jacket.

' . . . For one thing, tha's to be able to read and write before they'll set thi on. And for another, they wouldn't have a weedy little twat like thee.'

D. H. Lawrence wrote stories, novels and plays about Nottinghamshire, where he was born and brought up. (He wrote about other things and places as well.) When he had Nottinghamshire people talking, he nearly always tried to give an idea of the dialect in his writing. In this extract from Lawrence's play *The Daughter-in-Law*, Mrs Purdy has come to visit Mrs Gascoigne with some difficult news:

MRS GASCOIGNE:	An' how have yer all bin keeping'?
MRS PURDY:	Oh, very nicely—except our Bertha.
MRS GASCOIGNE:	Is she poorly, then?
MRS PURDY:	That's what I com ter tell yer. I niver knowed a word on't till a Sat'day, nor niver noticed a thing. Then she says to me, as white as a sheet, 'I've been sick

every morning, Mother,' an' it com across me like a shot from a gun. I sunk down i' that chair an' couldna fetch a breath.— An' me as prided myself! I've often laughed about it, an' said I was thankful my children had all turned out so well, lads an' wenches as well, an' said it was a'cause they was all got of a Sunday—their father was too drunk a'Saturday, an' too tired o'wik-days. An' it's a fact, they've all turned out well, for I'd allers bin to chappil. Well, I've said it for a joke, but now it's turned on me. I'd better ha' kep' my tongue still.

JOE: It's not me, though, missis. I wish it wor.

MRS PURDY: There's no occasions to ma'e gam' of it neither, as far as I can see. The youngest an' the last of 'em as I've got, an' a lass as I liked, for she's simple, but she's good-natured, an' him a married man. Thinks I to myself, 'I'd better go to's mother, she'll ha'e more about 'er than's new wife—for she's a stuck-up piece o' goods as ever trod.'

MRS GASCOIGNE: Why, what d'yer mean?

MRS PURDY: I mean what I say—an' there's no denyin' it. That girl—well, it's nigh on breakin' my heart, for I'm that short o' breath. (*Sighs.*) I'm sure!

MRS GASCOIGNE: Why, don't yer say what yer mean?

MRS PURDY: I've said it, haven't I? There's my gal gone four months wi' childt to your Luther.

MRS GASCOIGNE: Nay, nay, nay, missis! You'll never ma'e me believe it.

MRS PURDY: Glad would I be if I nedna. But I've gone through it all since Sat'day on. I've wanted to break every bone in 'er body—an' I've said I should on'y be happy if I was scraightin' at 'er funeral—an' I've said I'd wring his neck for 'im. But it doesn't alter it—there it is—an' there it will be. An' I s'll be a grandmother where my heart heaves, an' maun drag a wastrel baby through my old age. An' it's neither a cryin' nor a laughin' matter, but it's a matter of a girl wi' child, an' a man six week married.

You've probably heard of the book *Of Mice and Men* by the American writer, John Steinbeck. If you haven't read it, you should. The two main characters are George and Lennie, wandering ranch-hands. One Saturday night George goes into town, leaving Lennie on the ranch. Lennie is talking to Crooks, the black stable-hand. Lennie is big, slow and a bit simple.

Crooks's voice grew soft and persuasive. 'S'pose George don't come back no more. S'pose he took a powder and just ain't coming back. What'll you do then?'

Lennie's attention came gradually to what had been said. 'What?' he demanded.

'I said s'pose George went into town tonight and you never heard of him no more.' Crooks pressed forward some kind of private victory. 'Just s'pose that,' he repeated.

'He won't do it,' Lennie cried. 'George wouldn't do nothing like that. I been with George a long time. He'll come back to-night . . . '. But the doubt was too much for him. 'Don't you think he will?'

Crooks face lighted with pleasure in his torture. 'Nobody can't tell what a guy'll do,' he observed calmly. 'Le's say he wants to come back and can't. S'pose he gets killed or hurt so he can't come back.'

Lennie struggled to understand. 'George won't do nothing like that,' he repeated. 'George is careful. He won't get hurt. He ain't never been hurt, 'cause he's careful.'

'Well, s'pose, jus' s'pose he don't come back. What'll you do then?'

Lennie's face wrinkled with apprehension. 'I don' know. Say, what you doin' anyways?' he cried. 'This ain't true. George ain't got hurt.'

Crooks bored in on him. 'Want me ta tell ya what'll happen? They'll take ya to the booby hatch. They'll tie ya up with a collar, like a dog.'

Suddenly Lennie's eyes centred and grew quiet and mad. He stood up and walked dangerously towards Crooks. 'Who hurt George?' he demanded.

Crooks saw the danger as it approached him. He edged back on his bunk to get out of the way. 'I was just supposin', ' he said. 'George ain't hurt. He's all right. He'll be back all right.'

Lennie stood over him. 'What you supposin' for? Ain't nobody goin' to suppose no hurt to George.'

Crooks removed his glasses and wiped his eyes with his fingers. 'Jus' set down,' he said. 'George ain't hurt.'

Lennie growled back to his seat on the nail-keg. 'Ain't nobody goin' to talk no hurt to George,' he grumbled.

Crooks said gently: 'Maybe you can see now. You got George. You *know* he's goin' to come back. S'pose you didn't have nobody. S'pose you couldn't go into the bunk-house and play rummy 'cause you was black. How'd you like that? S'pose you had to sit out here an' read books. Sure you could play horseshoes till it got dark, but then you got to read books. Books ain't no good. A guy needs somebody—to be near him.' He whined: 'A guy goes nuts if he ain't got nobody. Don't make no difference who the guy is, long's he's with you. I tell ya,' he cried, 'I tell ya a guy gets too lonely an' he gets sick.'

The next piece, by Sandra Herridge, a London schoolgirl, is a complete story set in Jamaica. See how Sandra, like John Steinbeck and Barry Hines, uses SE for her narrative, and another dialect (in this case Jamaican creole) for the dialogue.

Mouta Massy

It was the day when the Common Entrance Examination results were coming out. Most of the people in Sherwood were hurrying to the Post Office to buy a newspaper.

Miss May flicked the latch of her gate, stole a last glance at herself through the glass of her bedroom window and then started her way to Sherwood crossroads, where the Post Office was. On her way there she met Miss Maty, one of Sherwood's commonest chatter-boxes.

Unlike Miss May, who was well-spoken and who looked quite neat, Miss Maty mixed her English with her own Jamaican way of speaking. She was wearing a pink roll-sleeve blouse, a yellow pleated skirt that had banana stain all over the front, and a kata on her head. She was carrying a bucket of water, but when she saw Miss May she put it down on the roadside, leaving only the kata on her head. She was preparing to gossip.

People in the district teased her by saying that the quickest way to spread news around the place was to tell Miss Maty. Because of her great liking to exercise her lips, they nicknamed her 'Mouta Massy'. Her excuse for being so nosey was that she lived all by herself and so when she got an opportunity to gossip there wasn't any harm in that. But the gossiping lips of Miss Maty often got her in difficult situations. That morning when she met Miss May was one of the many occasions.

MOUTA MASSY

by

SANDRA HERRIDGE

MISS MAY: Good morning Miss Maty, how are you this morning?

MISS MATY: Mi aright May. Weh yu going?

MISS MAY: I'm just going to the Post Office to buy a Glena*.

MISS MATY: Eh! eh! Yuh ton big shot ova night. Is only backra reading Glena nowadays.

MISS MAY: Don't be like that Miss Maty, I'm a working woman and I have all the rights in the world to read the papers when I want to!

MISS MATY: Sarry Miss May, but mi neva know dat yuh read al papers. Mi should've guessed—anyway, yuh are de posh type, only chat like mi when yuh angry.

MISS MAY: I don't always read the papers, but today is special you know. The results of the Common Entrance exam are coming out. I wonder if Sonia passed. She worked hard and the teacher told me that she have a good chance.

MISS MATY: Tek my advice, if shi pass nuh mek she goh to the same school as Jeanie gal Donna. Mi hear dat she bright in har lessons, but she don't have any manners whatsoever. Your pickney will have a good chance as long as shi nuh mingle wid dat gal. All shi tink about is ramping an' enjoying harself. An' har poor Muma, boy, sometimes mi heart grief fi de woman. Yuh know har pregnant sister was like dat. Every single night ena row shi used to go dance hall, an' stay till late. An' what about Jeanie's sister? Mi hear dat shi runnaway from home . . . An' . . . an' . . .

MISS MAY: Aright! Aright!!! Aright Miss Maty. Yuh making yuh mouth fly like cabbage ena put! Cho man! People don't have no secret in disa place. Yuh know bout people's background than dem know demselves. I don't have time to labrish wid yuh! Mi gane!

*Glena—Jamaican weekly newspaper.

MISS MATY: Wait fi mi! Mi deh com wid yuh!

MISS MAY: I do not wish to walk or talk with you Miss Maty. All a person need to lose their dignity is a bit of your lips, and anyway I haven't got time to wait until you go home and change.

MISS MATY: But mi not going home, mi coming like this.

MISS MAY: What?! People don't go to Sherwood crossroads like that!

MISS MATY: But mi not going to Sherwood crossroads. Mi will turn back halfway. Mi upset yuh, so mi will com and just keep yuh company.

MISS MAY: It's really nice of you Miss Maty, but you really don't have to.

MISS MATY: But I want to Miss May.

It wasn't until that moment that Miss Maty looked down. 'What are you going to do with the bucket? Miss Maty! Look at your feet! Them dying to wash! Look how the mud peeping from between your toes like peeping tam.' 'Oh no! I forgot to wash off mi feet. Mi slipped in a puddle when mi was helping up the bucket,' said Miss Maty.

A sudden, but somehow splendid idea flashed into Miss Maty's head. She ran to a nearby banana tree, tore a dry banana leaf from it and used the water from the bucket, with the leaf, to wash her muddy feet. She followed behind Miss May, telling her how sorry she was for making her lose her temper. She told Miss May that when she was a little girl her mother used to give her pepper and rice to stop her from chatting so much. Then she suddenly confessed that what she told Miss May about Miss Jeanie's daughter wasn't positively true. 'Mi tink Melva tell mi, mi not sure, but you know she don't like Jeanie already. They did fight at pipeside an' tore off each other's blouses. It was a shame to see two grown women going on like dat. Mind yuh, mi wasn't there. I went to market, but from what I heard it was disgraceful,' remarked Miss Maty.

'Miss Maty, your lips are drifting again. If Jeanie and Melva had a fight, that's none of your business! No wonder people call you "Mouta Massy". Anyway, we soon reach Sherwood crossroads, aren't you turning back?' asked Miss May. 'Mi reach too far already, soh I might as well come all the way. Mi will go an' visit Miss Margaret, we haven't had chat fi ages,' answered Miss Maty.

When they reached Sherwood Content (another name for the crossroads) Miss May went to get the newspaper and Miss Maty wandered off to gossip with a group of women whose daughers failed the exam. She talked and talked; one by one the people were leaving. Before long Miss Maty was standing barefooted, alone and sad on the piping hot Post Office step.

Miss May was nowhere to be seen so Miss Maty went home sadly.

Sonia did pass the exam and so did Donna. They were both sent to a nearby school in Falmouth. Both Miss May and Miss Jeanie were very proud of their daughters. As for Miss Maty, she continued to be a gossiper and found herself in many other embarassing situations.

Here are two poems by Julie Roberts, also in Jamaican. Julie now goes to college in London.

No Justice

We nah get justice inna dis ya Babylon,
We affee seek our justice outta Babylon,
We mus' return to Africa our righteous
    blessed land,
'Cause Babylonians' present system ah get
    way outta han',
Dem always accusing we fah wat we nevva
    don',
Trying fe teach WE! right fram wrang.
We tell dem seh we innocent but dey dou't
    our word,
Dem tek us inna court an' mek we look
    absurd,
We try tell dem seh Rasta no tief,
But dey dou't us still, dem still don't
    beleev!

False Rasta Strictly!!!

Hey you false Rasta out dere!
'Bout seh you ah locks up yuh hair —
You don't even know what locks is all
    about.
You tink is new fashon jus' com' out?
You don't even deal in the praising of Jah!
You is like de wolf, you know sah!
All when you ah hail I an' I
You say, 'Hell low' but nat 'Heaven high'.
You know notting 'bout Rastafari,
But ah wear de collas of Selassie I.

You want put dong yuh head,
An' tun true dread,
An' stap all dose bad ways,
An' give Jah Jah good praise!

If you are true,
Dis doesn't apply to you.
        One time!

Unless you happen to be Jamaican yourself, you will have found things in the
poems and the story you have just read
which you don't understand. Don't worry
about that; there is a list of dialect words
and spellings at the end of the chapter.
But please don't look at that list until you
have tried the activity on pages 44–45.

Cockney is the dialect of most people
who live in London. Over the years and
centuries, Cockney has suffered, maybe
more than any other English dialect, from
people being rude and ignorant about it.
Because of this, many Cockney speakers
feel a bit ashamed of their language. They
have been told that it is incorrect to say 'I
don't know nothing', it is lazy to 'drop an
h', and that Cockney is only good for
music-hall jokes, rhymes and slang. This

kind of prejudice, apart from being wrong
in the first place, is particularly odd when
you think that Standard English developed out of Cockney. To put it more
exactly, the East Midlands dialect of
English in the middle ages, which included
London speech, was the basis from which
richer, more educated people began to
differ in the way they spoke, to try to
distinguish themselves from the common
people. The educated people, because of
their education, had words in their
vocabulary which the common people
didn't know about. Of course, there's
nothing wrong with having a wide, educated vocabulary. That's a good thing. But
later on the educated people began to say
that their language was correct, and other
forms of English were incorrect. Because
many educated people were living in
London, they naturally compared their
language with the language of the poor
people of the same city. Later still, they
began to suggest that Cockney was somehow not capable of saying things which
are complicated, educated, moving or
serious. As a result of this, it's quite hard
to find examples of written Cockney which
are not songs, jokes or rhymes. However,
here is one example. A man called
Sheckles is making a speech and propos-
ing a toast at a wedding, about 90 years
ago.

'I ain't much of a speaker,' said Sheckles,
when everyone was quiet, 'an' it ain't in me
ter make a long fandangle. But I hev give
away terday a m'iden to a man—which
they're ole frien's both, though young other-
wise or comparatively so—an' I've took on
meself as a giver-away the dooties o' thet
parient who is, so ter speak, a time-expired
man in the realms o' glory .... The poet
sez, when somethin's whatsername we what
d'yer call it mingle, an' I'm o' the syme
opinion. There's a deal o' what I call
mootual trust like abart a weddin'. The man
'e sez: " 'Ere's a woman as I ain't know'd
long, but who I like instinctive. Fer all I
know, she may turn art a reg'lar art an' art
'ot 'un, or a right-darn good 'un. Anyway,
I'll tyke 'er an' make the best on 'er." An'

the woman she sez, "I'm nuts on him." Jest thet. But it means a lot. She don't weigh 'im up. Not she! She tykes 'im fer better or wuss, wi' the long odds on 'is bein' wuss. She's nuts on 'im—thet's ernough fer 'er .... I ain't a married man meself, through not ever 'avin bin pop'lar wi' the lydies, but I've often thort I'd like ter be one —thet's str'ight. Don't laugh. P'r'aps you've felt a bit lonely yerself sometimes when you've bin settin' over yer fire, an' yer pipe wont drawr, an' yer back's cold .... I know I hev. An' so I say: 'Ere's luck an' health an' long life an' 'appiness ter the man an' woman as I've give away ter one another terday. May they always enj'y life, an' never 'ave no quarrels, trustin' in the good Lord, an' buckin' up fer theirselves when times is bad.'

Old Sheckles blew his nose and grinned vacuously.

'Let 'er go,' he said. And the toast was drunk with acclamation.

Our last example of dialect writing is from Dorset. William Barnes (1801—86) lived and died in Dorset, and wrote poems in the Dorset dialect about the rural community which he was a part of. Here is a poem about Christmas. (When a vowel has two dots above it, as in *meäke*, it has to be pronounced separately from the vowel before it.)

Keepen up o' Chris'mas

An' zoo you didden come athirt,
To have zome fun last night: how wer't?
Vor we'd a-work'd wi' all our might
To scour the iron thigs up bright,
An' brush'd an' scrubb'd the house all
    drough;
An' brought in vor a brand, a plock

O' wood so big's an uppèn-stock,
An' hung a bough o' misseltoo,
An' ax'd a merry friend or two,
    To keepèn up o' Chris'mas.

An' there wer wold an' young; an' Bill,
Soon after dark, stalk'd up vrom mill.
An' when he wer a-comèn near,
He whissled loud vor me to hear;
Then roun' my head my frock I roll'd
An' stood in orcha'd like a post,
To meäke en think I wer a ghost.
But he wer up to't, an' did scwold
To vind me stannèn in the cwold,
    A keepèn up o' Chris'mas.

We play'd at forfeits, an' we spun
The trencher roun', an' meäde such fun!
An' had a geäme o' dree-ceärd loo,
An' then begun to hunt the shoe.
An' all the wold vo'k zittèn near,
A-chattèn roun' the vier pleäce,
Did smile in woone another's feäce,
An' sheäke right hands wi' hearty cheer,
An' let their left hands spill their beer,
    A keepèn up o' Chris'mas.

1) Try some dialect writing of your own. The dialect you choose is up to you; choose the one you know best, the one you have most control over. If you're writing a story, you may decide to put the narrative in SE and the dialogue in another dialect. If you write a short play, the stage directions should probably be in SE, the speeches in dialect. (Of course, that will depend on who the characters are.) With poetry, you may decide to try the whole thing in dialect.

2) Look back at the examples of dialect writing above.

a) Make a list of all the words which do not occur in SE, e.g. *tha, scraightin'*. Try to think of words in SE which mean roughly the same thing as the dialect words. Write the SE and the dialect words next to each other:

(Yorkshire) tha: (SE) you
(Nottinghamshire) scraightin':
    (SE) crying

(There is a complete list of the dialect words, with their SE meanings, at the end of the chapter. But don't look there until you've tried the activity yourself.)

b) Make a list of the occasions when the dialect writing uses grammar which is different from the grammar which SE would normally use. By *grammar* here we mean the way the words are arranged in sentences, the kinds of forms and endings words have, the way questions are asked, the way negative words like *not, never, no one* are put into sentences. Write down the grammar which you think SE would use, next to the examples of dialect grammar:

(Jamaica) We nah get justice:
(SE) We get no justice
(California) I been with George a long time:
(SE) I've been with George a long time
(Yorkshire) . . . have I to tell thi why?:
(SE) . . do I have to tell you why?

c) Write down all the words which have been spelt differently from normal, to give an idea of the way they are pronounced in the dialect. Put down the usual spellings next to the dialect spellings.

(Cockney) ter: (SE) to
(Dorset) zome: (SE) some

(Some of the most unusual spellings are in the list at the end of the chapter.)

3) Here are 10 questions about dialect. You can use them in at least four ways:

— have a group discussion on dialect, and use some or all of the questions;
— interview someone else about dialect, and use some or all of the questions;
— answer the questions in writing;
— use the questions as the basis for a continuous piece of writing on dialect. If you want a title for the piece, call it *Dialect as Part of my Language.*

A Questionnaire

a) Do you have different ways of speaking at different times and places? How would you describe them? When do you speak in these different ways, and what sort of people are you with when you do? (e.g. at home, to teachers, to friends, to your grandparents, etc.)

b) Do you think there is such a thing as proper English? Can you describe it? Who speaks it?

c) Are there ever times when you feel uncertain of yourself because of the way you're speaking? Can you give an example?

d) Do you think you have a dialect? When do you use it? Do you enjoy using it?

e) If your normal dialect is not SE, are there still times when you prefer using SE?

f) Are there things that you can say in dialect that you can't say in any other way? What sort of things?

g) If you talk in dialect at home, how do your parents react?

h) If you talk in dialect in class, how do your teachers react?

i) Do you think that your dialect should be used in the classroom? In what way?

j) Do you think there are any advantages or disadvantages in having a dialect?

Style

The first of the 10 questions touched on something which is rather different from dialect, though connected with it. You might decide that you only use one dialect, but that you still talk differently at different times and places, depending on who you're with. In fact, everyone, whether they normally use only one or more than one dialect, speaks in different ways at different times.

On the way home one evening you see a street fight.
1) You tell your friend about it.
2) You tell your parents about it.
3) The police appeal for witnesses to the fight. You go to the police station and report what you have seen to a police officer.

Work out how you would speak in these three different situations. The best way to do this is in pairs, acting out the conversations.

The differences between these three ways of speaking are differences of *style.*

You use different styles of language because different people are listening to you. You think of those people in different ways. You have an idea of what they will be interested in, what they will approve of, what sort of language they expect from you.

You're asking for money. But 'you' this time is a number of different people:

1) a tramp begging the price of a cup of tea;
2) yourself, asking one of your parents for money to go out to the cinema/disco/football match;
3) someone collecting for charity;
4) a shop assistant adding up the price of goods and charging the customer;
5) a rent-collector talking to a tenant who hasn't paid rent for 10 weeks.

Either act out these short scenes in pairs, or write them down. Best of all, act them out first, so you feel confident about them, and then write them down. When we say *act*, we don't *necessarily* mean stand up and walk round the room. If that's not possible, you can get into the part just sitting where you are. Still, it's easier if you can move.

Style in language has got a lot to do with power. The differences between the five people asking for money in the last activity are differences in the amount of power behind them when they're doing the asking. How much power they have will affect the kinds of words they use, their tone of voice, whether they are careful or casual, uncertain or confident, in what they say.

Try to imitate the following styles of language:

1) sports commentary on television;
2) a political speech;
3) selling umbrellas or cheap jewellery on upturned orange boxes in the street;
4) gossip between adults who know each other well;
5) a teacher trying to get a lesson going with a difficult class;
6) children playing together a game which they all know (jacks, two-ball, hop-scotch, marbles, conkers).

Children's language

Children have their own language, sometimes a dialect, sometimes a style, sometimes a mixture of both. This language is different from the language they use to teachers, parents, to the adult world. It's the language of rhymes, games, of secret words, of oaths, codes and truces. All children hear it, most children use it, and most people forget about it when they are no longer children. The special language of children has thousands of variations, depending on which part of the English-speaking world you go to. Here are a few children's rhymes.

1) Don't go to granny's any more, more, more.
   There's a big fat copper at the door, door, door.
   Well, he'll fetch you by the collar
   You owe him half a dollar
   So don't go to granny's any more, more, more.

2) Kent County Council, K.C.C.,
   They asked me to come to tea.
   'Have you got a cold, sir?'
   'No sir, why sir?'
   'You don't look very well, sir,
   Let me hear you cough.' (*Someone
     coughs.*)
   'Very bad indeed, sir, better go to bed.
   How many blankets do you want?'
   (*Someone gives a number. The number is
   counted round the group. Whoever the
   number arrives at has to start the rhyme
   again.*)

3) One potato, two potato, three potato,
     four,
   Five potato, six potato, seven potato,
     more.

4) Lulu had a baby, she called it sunny Jim
   She took it to the swimming baths
   To see if it could swim.
   It sank to the bottom and floated to the
     top
   Lulu got excited and grabbed it by the
   Cockles and mussels, two and six a jar
   If you do not like them stick them up
     your
   Ask no questions, tell no lies
   Have you ever seen a policeman doing
     up his
   Flies are a nuisance, fleas are even worse
   And that is the end of Lulu's dirty
     verse.

5) I'm a girl guide dressed in blue
   These are the actions I must do:
   Salute to the Captain
   Bow to the Queen,
   And show my knickers to the football
     team.

6) On top of spaghetti, all covered with
     cheese
   I lost my poor meatball, when somebody
     sneezed.
   It rolled on the table, and on to the floor
   And then my poor meatball rolled
     outside the door.
   It rolled out in the garden, and under a
     bush
   And then my poor meatball was covered
     in slush.
   So if you have spaghetti, all covered in
     cheese
   Hold on to your meatball, 'cause some-
     body might sneeze.

7) Two little monkeys jumping on a bed
   One fell off and hurt his head.
   One called the doctor, doctor said,
   'No more monkeys jumping on bed.'

Rhymes are often used for games like
skipping and two-ball, or for picking up
teams for football, cricket or rounders.
Often, rhymes have long histories, and get
updated regularly by the names of new
film or TV stars, or by recent political
events.

When children are going to play a game, one might say quickly, 'Bags I go in first!' or 'Bags first base!' or 'Bags I bowling!' Someone else will say 'Bags I second!', and positions in the game will be decided according to who has bagsed them. Children are usually happy to accept the rules of bagsing, although sometimes there may be arguments over who has bagsed what. (Some people say *bagged*, but we used to say *bagsed* when we were kids.)

If children want a rest from a game, or a truce from a fight, they might say *fains* or *fainites* or *vainites*, and the others will usually leave them alone for a while, or let them have a rest. *Vainites* gives you protection, as long as you don't use it too often. There are different words which mean the same things as *bags* or *fainites*, depending on where you grow up. Instead of *bags*, you might say *chaps* in Scotland, *ferry* in west Yorkshire, and *jigs it* in Manchester. Instead of *fainites* you might say *barley* in Liverpool, Lancashire, north and west Wales and eastern Scotland, *cree* in south-east Wales and Gloucestershire, or *skinch* in Northumberland and Durham.

Children's truce words in Britain

Back-slang

In different parts of Britain, children use a secret vocabulary called back-slang. It was originally used by barrow-boys and street-sellers, and in greengrocers' and butchers' shops where it was spoken so that the customer should not understand what was being said. Here are two different kinds of back-slang:

1) Ouray eachtayeray isay oolfay.
2) Agi lagike thagat bagoy wagith bragown hagair.

You can probably work out quite easily what these sentences mean when they're written down. But you can see how difficult they would be to understand when said, unless you knew the code. That's the point of them, of course.

---

1) Describe any kind of back-slang or other secret code language which you have used. How did it work? Can you remember any occasions when parents or teachers tried to stop you understanding what they were saying? Any occasions when you tried to do the same to them?

2) Write a short message or conversation in a code language. Either use a code you know, or make one up. Explain the rules of the code and, if you like, give a translation into normal English.

Here are the dialect words and phrases, slang words, and some unusual spellings which you may not recognize, from the pieces of dialect writing in this chapter. The SE words and phrases next to them sometimes mean only roughly the same thing.

Yorkshire	SE
Tha	you
thi	you

Nottinghamshire	SE
ma'e gam'	make a joke
scraightin'	crying, howling
maun	must
wastrel	stray, unwanted

California	SE
took a powder	went off, disappeared
booby-hatch	mental hospital
nail-keg	nail-barrel

Jamaica (Mouta Massey)	SE
kata	folded cloth
backra	snobbish people or white people
mek	let
pickney	child
ramping	playing around
fi	for
Cho man!	For God's sake!
labrish	gossip
Mi gane!	I'm going!
Mi deh com	I am coming
at pipeside	by the water pipe

Jamaica (No Justice)	SE
dis ya	this here
affee	have to
ah get	is getting
fah	for
fe	to
seh	that
Rasta no tief	Rastafarians don't steal

Jamaica (No Justice)	SE
dis ya	this here
affee	have to
ah get	is getting
fah	for
fe	to
seh	that
Rasta no tief	Rastafarians don't steal

Jamaica (False Rasta Strictly!!!)	SE
'Bout seh you ah locks up yuh hair	What's all this about doing your hair up in locks?
Jah	God, Jehovah
sah	sir
All when you ah hail I and I	Whenever you greet me
Rastafari	the Rastafarian religion
ah wear	you're wearing
Selassie I	King Haile Selassie
dong	down
true dread	really serious about the Rastafarian religion

Cockney	SE
fandangle	fuss
art an' art 'ot 'un	regular tearaway
right-darn	downright
buckin' up fer theirselves	looking after themselves

Dorset	SE
Keepen up	celebrating
athirt	across
drough	through
brand	piece of firewood
uppen-stock	horse-mounting-block
wold	old
frock	smock
meäke	make
en	him
trencher	wooden plate
meäde	made
geäme	game
dree-ceärd loo	card game like whist
vo'k	folk
zitten	sitting
vier pleäce	fire place
feäce	face
sheäke	shake

50

4

English has a History

In the last chapter we looked at quite a number of varieties and changes within the English language. Let's look now at an example of a story which has changed in time, and changed from place to place as well.

Selling ballads

The Maid Freed from the Gallows

A girl is going to be hanged. Just before she is due to die, she appeals to her father to pay the money which would set her free. Her father refuses. Then she appeals to her mother, then to her brother, then to her sister. They all refuse. At last the girl appeals to her lover to pay the money to set her free. Her lover says 'Yes', he pays the money, the girl is set free, and away they go together. A simple story. In fact,

this particular story is nearly always told in the form of a ballad. Ballads are songs which tell stories. This ballad has spread all over the world, and its story is sung in many different languages. It has been going for hundreds of years; no one knows exactly how many. Here is a version of it which was written down just over 200 years ago, and comes from Kent. It's called *The Maid Freed from the Gallows*.

'O good Lord Judge, and sweet Lord
   Judge,
Peace for a little while!
Methinks I see my own father,
Come riding by the stile.

'Oh father, oh father, a little of your gold,
And likewise of your fee!
To keep my body from yonder grave,
And my neck from the gallows-tree!'

'None of my gold now shall you have,
Nor likewise of my fee;
For I am come to see you hang'd
And hangèd you shall be.'

'Oh good Lord Judge, and sweet Lord
   Judge,
Peace for a little while!
Methinks I see my own mother,
Come riding by the stile.

'Oh mother, oh mother, a little of your
   gold,
And likewise of your fee,
To keep my body from yonder grave,
And my neck from the gallows-tree!'

'None of my gold now shall you have,
Nor likewise of my fee;
For I am come to see you hang'd
And hangèd shall you be.'

'Oh good Lord Judge, and sweet Lord
   Judge,
Peace for a little while!
Methinks I see my own brother,
Come riding by the stile.

'Oh brother, oh brother, a little of your
   gold,
And likewise of your fee,
To keep my body from yonder grave,
And my neck from the gallows-tree!'

'None of my gold now shall you have,
Nor likewise of my fee;
For I am come to see you hang'd
And hangèd you shall be.'

'Oh good Lord Judge, and sweet Lord
   Judge,
Peace for a little while!
Methinks I see my own sister,
Come riding by the stile.

'Oh sister, oh sister, a little of your gold,
And likewise of your fee,
To keep my body from yonder grave,
And my neck from the gallows-tree!'

'None of my gold now shall you have,
Nor likewise of my fee;
For I am come to see you hang'd
And hangèd you shall be.'

'Oh good Lord Judge, and sweet Lord
   Judge,
Peace for a little while!
Methinks I see my own true-love,
Come riding by the stile.

'Oh true-love, oh true-love, a little of your
   gold,
And likewise of your fee,
To keep my body from yonder grave,
And my neck from the gallows-tree!'

'Some of my gold now shall you have,
And likewise of your fee;
For I am come to see you saved,
And saved you shall be.'

This ballad is easy for us to understand,
although it is more than 200 years old. Languages change very slowly. Even so, there
are some words in it which we would not
normally use today, in songs or in speech,
unless we were deliberately imitating an
old-fashioned style. Look back through the
ballad and decide which words these are.

Here is a version of the same ballad from
Scotland.

'Hold your hand, Lord Judge,' she says,
'Yet hold it a little while;
Methinks I see my ain dear father
Coming wandering many a mile.

'O have you brought me gold, father?
Or have you brought me fee?
Or are you come to save my life
From off this gallows-tree?'

'I have not brought you gold, daughter,
Nor have I brought you fee,
But I am come to see you hang'd
As you this day shall be.'

The verses carry on in this way for the
girl's mother, brother and sister. Then,

'Hold your hand, Lord Judge,' she says,
'Yet hold it a little while;
Methinks I see my ain dear lover
Coming wandering many a mile.

'O have you brought me gold, true-love?
Or have you brought me fee?
Or are you come to save my life
From off this gallows-tree?'

'I have not brought you gold, true-love,
Nor yet have I brought you fee,
But I am come to save thy life
From off this gallows-tree.'

'Gae hame, gae hame, father,' she says,
'Gae hame and saw yer seed;
And I wish not a pickle of it may grow up,
But the thistle and the weed.

'Gae hame, gae hame, gae hame, mother,
Gae hame and brew yer yill;
And I wish the girds may a' loup off,
And the Deil spill a' yer yill.

'Gae hame, gae hame, gae hame, brother,
Gae hame and lie with yer wife;
And I wish that the first news I may hear
That she has tane your life.

'Gae hame, gae hame, sister,' she says,
'Gae hame and sew yer seam;
I wish that the needle-point may break,
And the craws pyke out yer een.'

ain — own	pickle — grain	Deil — Devil
Gae — go	yill — ale	tane — taken
hame — home	girds—	craws—crows
saw — sow	handles	pyke — pick
yer — your	a' — all	een — eyes
	loup — jump	

Stories and ballads travel widely. Here is the same basic story, being told partly as a folk-tale and partly as a song, in Jamaica. Here the girl has a name—Saylan (another spelling of Sally Ann).

There was a man have two daughter. One of the daughter belongs to the wife an' one belongs to the man. An' the wife no love for the man daughter, so they drive her away.

An' she get a sitivation at ten shillings a week, an' the work is to look after two horses an' to cut dry grass for them.

An' every night she put two bundles of dry grass in the stable.

An' the mother was very grudgeful of the sitivation that she got.

An' one night she carry her own daughter to the pastur' an' they cut two bundles of green grass. An' they go secretly to the horse manger an' take out the dry grass an' put the green grass in its place.

So, the horse eat it, an' in the morning they dead.

An' the master of that horse is a sailor.

The sailor took the girl who caring the horse to hang her.

An' when he get to the spot a place to hang her he take this song:—

'Mourn, Saylan, mourn oh! Mourn, Saylan, mourn;
I come to town to see you hang, hang, you mus' be hang.'

An' the gal cry to her sister an' brother an' lover, an' they give her answer:

'Sister, you bring me some silver?' 'No my child, I bring you none.'

'Brother, you bring me some gold?' 'No my child, I bring you none.'

'Lover, you bring me some silver?' 'Yes my dear, I bring you some.'

'Lover, you bring me some gold?' 'Yes my dear, I bring you some.

I come to town to see you save, save you mus' be saved.'

An' the lover bring a buggy an' carry her off an' save her life at last.

An' the mumma say:— 'You never better, tuffa.'

caring—taking care off
You never better—you will never be good for anything
tuffa—a word which imitates spitting

Finally, here is a song of the twentieth century, by the great black American folk-singer Leadbelly, called *The Gallis Pole*. You should be able to recognize the story, although it's changed a lot; for one thing, the person about to be hanged is now a man.

Leadbelly

'Papa, did you bring me any silvo?
Papa, did you bring me any gold?
What did you bring me, dear Papo,
To keep me from the gallis pole?
Yes, what did you,
Yes, what did you,
What did you bring me to keep me from
  the gallis pole?'

(*Spoken*)
In olden times years ago,
When you put a man in prison
Behind the bars in jailhouse,
If he had fifteen or twenty-five or thirty
  dollars,
You could save him from the gallis pole
  'cause they gonna hang him
If he don't bring up a little money.
Ev'ybody would come to the jailhouse,
The boy up the side of the jail,
He was married, too,
Ask for who bring him somep'n.
Father come first, here come his
  mother . . .

(*Sung*)
'Mother, did you bring me any silvo?
Mother, did you bring me any gold?
What did you bring me, dear Motho,
To keep me from the gallis pole?
Yes, what did you,
Yes, what did you,
What did you bring me to keep me from
  the gallis pole?'

'Son, I brought you some silvo,
Son, I brought you some gold,
Son, I brought you ev'ything
To keep you from the gallis pole.
Yes, I brought it,
Yes, I brought it,
I brought you, to keep you from the gallis
  pole.'

(*Spoken*)
Here come his wife, plow-points and old
  trace-chains,
Ev'thing in the world she could to get 'im
  outta jailhouse.
His wife brought all kinds a . . .

(*Sung*)
'Wife, did you bring me any silvo?
Wife, did you bring me any gold?
What did you bring me, dear wifey,
To keep me from the gallis pole?
Yes, what did you,
Yes, what did you,
What did you bring me, to keep me from
  the gallis pole?'

'Husband, I brought you some silvo,
Husband, I brought you some gold,
Husband, I brought you ev'ything
To keep you from the gallis pole.'

gallis pole—gallows
plow-points and old trace-chains
  —metal parts off the plough, which
    might be accepted instead of money

There are many reasons for the differences between these four versions of a simple story. There are differences of dialect. There are changes which the singers and story-tellers made themselves as the ballad travelled across the world. A twentieth-century ballad would not normally use words like *methinks, yonder* or *likewise*. On the other hand, ballads hold on tightly to some traditions, like the shape of their verses, the repeating choruses, the questions and answers.

---

1) Look again at the four versions of the ballad. What do all four have in common? What are the important differences between them? Differences or similarities may be in the actual story told, or in the way it is told (the kind of verse each version uses, the mixture of talking and singing). Try a piece of writing called *Four Versions of a Ballad.* Make it as detailed as you can.

2) Ballads are still alive and still changing. Write your own up-to-date version of *The Maid Freed from the Gallows.* You could change it to *The Girl Saved from the Firing-Squad* or *The Boy who Escaped the Electric Chair*, as you like. But keep some connections with the older versions. Notice how ballads very often use four-line verses, with a rhyme at the end of the second and fourth lines.

A modern ballad

Some of the energy and imagination which used to go into writing, selling and singing ballads now goes into pop- or rock-music. Here is a modern ballad, written and sung by Ian Dury. A lot of rock-music sounds American even if it isn't. An important thing about Ian Dury's songs is that they use his own dialect (Cockney) and don't apologise for it.

Ian Dury

My Old Man

>   My old man wore three-piece whistles, he
>   was never home for long
>   Drove a bus for London Transport, he
>   knew where he belonged.
>   Number eighteen down to Euston, double
>   decker move along,
>   double decker move along.
>   My old man.
>
>   Later on he drove a Roller, chaufferin' for
>   foreign men,
>   Dropped his aitches on occasion, said 'Cor
>   Blimey' now and then
>   Did the crossword in the *Standard* at the
>   airport in the rain,
>   at the airport in the rain.
>   My old man.
>
>   Wouldn't ever let his guvnors call him
>   Billy, he was proud.
>   Personal reasons make a difference, his
>   last boss was allowed.
>   P'rhaps he had to keep his distance, made
>   a racket when he rowed,
>   made a racket when he rowed.
>   My old man.
>
>   My old man was fairly han'some, he
>   smoked too many cigs,
>   Lived in one room in Victoria, he was tidy
>   in his digs.
>   Had to have an operation when his ulcer
>   got too big,
>   when his ulcer got too big.
>   My old man.
>
>   Seven years went out the window
>   We met as one to one.
>   Died before we'd done much talkin',
>   Relations had begun.
>   All the while we'd thought about each
>   other
>   All the best mate from your son,
>   all the best mate from your son.
>   My old man, my old man.'

whistles—suits   Roller—Rolls Royce
digs—lodgings

Three versions of a Bible story

The obvious way to see how English changes through time is to take pieces of writing from different centuries, and look at the differences between them. But an even better idea, to begin with, is to take one story which has appeared in English at different times and in different forms. The Bible has been translated into English many times, and in St Luke's gospel in the New Testament there is a story called *The Prodigal Son*. The first part of the story goes like this.

A man had two sons. One day, the younger son asked his father to give him the share of the property which he was due to inherit. His father did this, and a few days later the younger son went away to a distant country, where he wasted all his money by wild living. When he had no money left, there was a famine in the country, and he got a job feeding pigs. He was starving hungry, and at last he decided to go back to his father and ask to become one of his paid servants. He said to himself, 'Even my father's servants are better off than I am now.' So he went back, and his father, instead of being angry with him, was overjoyed to see him, welcomed him home, and organized a party to celebrate. The father ordered the best animal he had, a fattened-up calf, to be killed and cooked for the party.

Here is the next part of the story as it appears in the *New English Bible*, which was published in 1961.

Now the elder son was out on the farm; and on his way back, as he approached the house, he heard music and dancing. He called one of the servants and asked what it meant. The servant told him, 'Your brother has come home, and your father has killed the fatted calf because he has him back safe and sound.' But he was angry and refused to go in. His father came out and pleaded with him; but he retorted, 'You know how I have slaved for you all these years; I never once disobeyed your orders; and you never gave me so much as a kid, for a feast with my friends. But now that this son of yours turns up, after running through your money with his women, you kill the fatted calf for him.' 'My boy,' said the father, 'you are always with me, and everything I have is yours. How could we help celebrating this happy day? Your brother here was dead and has come back to life, was lost and is found.'

The most famous English translation of the Bible is the *King James Version*, which was published exactly 350 years before the piece you've just read, in 1611. Here is the same part of the prodigal son story in the *King James Version*.

Now his elder sonne was in the field, and as he came and drew nigh to the house, he heard musicke & dauncing, and he called one of the seruants, and asked what these things meant. And he said vnto him, Thy brother is come, and thy father hath killed the fatted calfe, because he hath receiued him safe and sound. And he was angry, and would not goe in: therefore his father came out, and intreated him. And he answering said to his father, Loe, these many yeeres doe I serue thee, neither transgressed I at any time thy commandement, and yet thou neuer gauest mee a kid, that I might make merry with my friends: but as soone as this thy sonne was come, which hath deuoured thy liuing with harlots, thou hast killed for him the fatted calfe. And he said vnto him, Sonne, thou are euer with me, and all that I haue is thine. It was meete that we should make merry, and be glad: for this thy brother was dead, and is aliue againe: and was lost, and is found.

Wycliffe's translation of the Bible

The first man to translate the whole Bible into English was John Wycliffe. Wycliffe lived in the fourteenth century; he died in 1384. Here is his translation of the same passage.

Forsoth his eldere sone was in the feeld, and whanne he cam and neighede to the hous, he herde a symfonye and a croude. And he clepide oon of the seruantis, and axide what thingis thes weren. And he seide to him, Thi brodir is comen, and thi fadir hath slayn a fat calf, for he resseyued him saf. Forsoth he was wroth, and wolde not entre: therfore his fadir yede out, bigan to preie him. And he answeringe to his fadir seide, Lo, so manye yeeris I serue to thee, and I brak neuere thi commaundement, thou hast neuere yovun a kyde to me, that I schulde ete largely with my frendis. But aftir that this thi sone, which deuouride his substaunce with hooris, cam, thou hast slayn to him a fat calf. And he seide to him, Sone, thou ert euere with me, and alle myne thingis ben thyne. Forsoth it bihofte to ete plenteously, and for to ioye: for this thi brother was deed, and lyuede ayeyn: he peryschide, and he is founden.

Not all of the differences between these three translations are due to changes in English. Some of the differences are there because the translators had different ideas about how best to put the story into English. Let's look at the first words in each version:

Now the elder son was out on the farm
(New English Bible)
Now his elder sonne was in the field
(King James Version)
Forsoth his eldere sone was in the feeld
(Wycliffe)

The *New English Bible* has the elder son *on the farm*. The two older versions have him *in the field*. Obviously, this is not because the word *field* has changed to *farm* in modern English. It hasn't. We still use both words. That difference is there because the *New English Bible* translators thought *farm* was more appropriate. But there are differences between the versions which are a result of changes in the language. There are spelling differences: *elder/eldere, son/sonne/sone,*

field/feeld. And Wycliffe's old word *Forsoth*, which meant *in truth* or *indeed*, has been replaced by *Now*, used in the weak way it often is at the beginning of sentences.

You probably found the *King James Version* quite easy to understand, and the *Wycliffe Version* hard to understand. Of course, this is because the *Wycliffe Version* is more than 200 years older than the *King James Version*, and English changed a lot during those 200 years. Here are the words in the two older versions which you may need help with:

King James Version
Thy—Your
intreated—begged
thee, thou—you
Loe—Now look!
transgressed—disobeyed
kid—young goat
harlots—prostitutes
meete—right and proper
Wycliffe Version
Forsoth—In truth
neighede—came close to
symfonye—musical instrument
croude—fiddle, violin
clepide—called
oon—one
axide—asked
thes—these
Thi—Your
resseyued—received
saf—safe
wroth—angry
yede—went
preie—beg
thee, thou—you
yovun—given
largely—plentifully
devouride—wasted
substaunce—goods, possessions
hooris—prostitutes, whores
slayn—killed
ert—are
ben—are
it bihofte—it was right
to ioye—to be merry
deed—dead
lyuede—came to life
ayeyn—again
peryschide—was lost

Another thing you have to get used to about the two older versions is that they use the letter *u* where modern English uses *v* (*seruants* and *euer* for *servants* and *ever*) and sometimes they use *v* where modern English uses *u* (*vnto* instead of *unto*). This only happened in writing; it did not affect the way the words were said.

Sometimes we can see words in the older versions which are basically the same as in the modern version, but have different endings (*hath* instead of *has, gavest* instead of *gave*).

Sometimes the older versions use words which are quite different from the word used in the same place in the modern version. This may be because the older words have changed their meaning (*largely* now means *mainly*, not *plentifully*), or because they sound out-of-date (like *slayn*), or because they have disappeared from the language altogether (like *clepide*). As we said before, the change may also be something to do with the translator.

---

1) Make a table of the words in any of the three versions which are basically the same, but are spelt differently or have different endings. You could set out the table like this:

New English Bible	King James Version	Wycliffe Version
son	sonne	sone
—	field	feeld etc.

2) Make another table of the words which are quite different in any of the different versions:

New English Bible	King James Version	Wycliffe Version
Now	Now	Forsoth
farm	field	feeld
approached	drew nigh to	neighede to etc.

Six English conversations

Here now are six bits of English dialogue, or conversation, which have been written down at various times during the last thousand years. They are not in chronological order; we've deliberately mixed them up.

A. *An inquisitive gentleman talking to a cab driver.*

'How old is that horse, my friend?' inquired Mr Pickwick, rubbing his nose with the shilling he had reserved for the fare.

'Forty-two,' replied the driver, eyeing him askant.

'What!' ejaculated Mr Pickwick, laying his hand upon his note-book. The driver reiterated his former statement. Mr Pickwick looked very hard at the man's face; but his features were immovable, so he noted down the fact forthwith.

'And how long do you keep him out at a time?' inquired Mr Pickwick, searching for further information.

'Two or three veeks,' replied the man.

'Weeks!' said Mr Pickwick in astonishment—and out came the note-book again.

'He lives at Pentonwil when he's at home,' observed the driver, coolly, 'but we seldom takes him home, on account of his veakness.'

'On account of his weakness!' reiterated the perplexed Mr Pickwick.

'He always falls down when he's took out o' the cab,' continued the driver, 'but when he's in it, we bears him up werry tight, and takes him in werry short, so as he can't werry well fall down; and we've got a pair o' precious large wheels on, so ven he does move, they run after him, and he must go on—he can't help it.'

B. *King Arthur, badly wounded, talking to three queens in a boat, and to one of his followers.*

'Now put me in to the barge,' sayd the kyng, and so he dyd softelye. And there receyved hym thre quenes wyth grete mornyng, and soo they sette hem down, and in one of their lappes kyng Arthur layed hys heed, and than that quene sayd, 'a dere broder! why have ye taryed so longe from me. Alas, this wounde on your heed hath caught overmoche colde.' And soo than they rowed from the londe, and syr bedwere behelde all tho ladyes goo from hym. Than syr bedwere cryed, 'a! my lord Arthur, what shal become of me now ye goo from me. And leve me here allone emonge myn enemyes?' 'Comfort thy self,' sayd the kyng, 'and doo as wel as thou mayst; for in me is no truste for to truste in. For I wyl in to the vale of auylyon, to hele me of my greuous wounde. And yf thou here neuer more of me, praye for my soule;' but ever the quenes and ladyes wepte and shryched that hit was pyte to here.

C. *A pickpocket and scoundrel (Autolicus) pretending he has just been beaten up, and conning an innocent passer-by (Clown)*

AUTOLICUS: Oh, that ever I was born!
CLOWN: I' th' name of me!
AUTOLICUS: Oh help me, help mee! Plucke but of theese ragges: and then, death, death.
CLOWN: Alacke poore soule, thou hast need of more rags to lay on thee, rather then have these off.
AUTOLICUS: Oh sir, the loathsomenesse of them offend mee, more than the stripes I have receiued, which are mightie ones and millions.

CLOWN: Alas poore man, a million of beating may come to a great matter.
AUTOLICUS: I am rob'd sir, and beaten: my money, and apparrell tane from me, and these detestable things put upon me.
CLOWN: What, by a horseman, or a footman?
AUTOLICUS: A footman (sweet sir) a footman.
CLOWN: Indeed, he should be a footman, by the garments he hath left with thee: If this be a horsemans Coate, it hath seene very hot service. Lende me thy hand, Ile helpe thee. Come, lend me thy hand.
AUTOLICUS: Oh good sir, tenderly, oh.
CLOWN: Alas, poor soule!
AUTOLICUS: Oh good sir, softly, good sir: I feare (sir) my shoulder-blade is out.
CLOWN: How now? Canst stand?
AUTOLICUS: Softly, deere sir: good sir, softly: you ha' done me a charitable office.
(Autolicus picks the Clown's pocket.)

D. *A pupil talking to a teacher.*

PUPIL: We cildra bidda e, eala lareow, þaet þu taece us sprecan rihte, forþam ungelaerede we sindon, and gewaemmodlice we sprecaþ.
MASTER: Hwaet wille ge sprecan?
PUPIL: Hwaet rece we hwaet we sprecan, buton hit riht spraec sy and behefe, naes idel oþþe fracod?
MASTER: Wille ge beon beswungen on leornunge?
PUPIL: Leofre is us beon beswungen for lare þaenne hit ne cunnan; ac we witan þe bilewitne wesan, and nellan onbelaedan swincgla us, buton þu bi togenydd fram us.

E. *A young gangster, The Boy, covering up a murder he has just committed.*

The Boy looked down at the body, spread-eagled like Prometheus, at the bottom of Frank's stairs. 'Good God,' Mr Prewitt said, 'how did it happen?'

The Boy said: 'These stairs have needed mending a long while. I've told Frank about it, but you can't make the bastard spend money.' He put his hand on the rail and pushed until it gave. The rotten wood lay across Spicer's body, a walnut-stained eagle couched over the kidneys.

'But that happened *after* he fell,' Mr Prewitt protested; his insinuating legal voice was tremulous.

'You've got it wrong,' the Boy said. 'You were here in the passage and you saw him lean his suitcase against the rail. He shouldn't have done that. The case was too heavy.'

'My God, you can't mix me up in this,' Mr Prewitt said. 'I saw nothing. I was looking in the soap dish, I was with Dallow.'

'You both saw it,' the Boy said. 'That's fine. It's a good thing we have a fine respectable lawyer like you on the spot. Your word will do the trick.'

Mr Prewitt and the Boy

F. *An uncle (Pandarus) visiting his niece (Criseyde) who is reading a book with some friends.*

> Quod Pandarus, 'Madame, God yow see,
> With al youre fayre book and compaignie!'
> Ey, uncle myn, welcome iwys,' quod she;
> And up she roos, and by the hond in hye
> She took hym faste, and seyde, 'This nyght thrie,
> To goode mot it turne, of yow I mette.'
> And with that word she down on bench hym sette.
>
> 'Ye, nece, yee shal faren wel the bet,
> If God wol, al this yeer,' quod Pandarus;
> 'But I am sorry that I have yow let
> To herken of youre book ye preysen thus.
> For Goddes love, what seith it? telle it us!
> Is it of love? O, som good ye me leere!'
> 'Uncle,' quod she, 'youre maistresse is nat here.'

---

1) When you have read these six bits of conversation carefully, try to decide which is the oldest, which is the next oldest, and so on, working through to the one you think is the most recent. Or start with the most recent one, and work backwards. When you've decided on your order, see if it agrees with our order, which we've put at the end of the chapter. You can also find translations there of the conversations you might have found difficult to understand.

2) Look again at conversations A to F. You know the order they were written in. You speak, and write, the English of the 1980s. Going backwards through time, you can see that the pieces get more and more different from modern English. Can you say how? This is a difficult activity, so these questions may help you:

— As the pieces get older, what words are used which have disappeared in modern English?

— As the pieces get older, how do the spellings change?

— Can you find words in the older pieces which we still use, but with a different meaning?

— Can you find sentences or phrases in the older pieces where the words are arranged in a different order from modern English?

— Can you find words or phrases which you understand, but which would sound really old-fashioned today?

3) Choose one of the conversations A to F, and try to write a piece of conversation of your own in that kind of English. Here is our attempt to write a few lines in the style of conversation C:

BEGGAR: Come hither, my friend. I would speke with thee.

RICH MAN: What businesse hast thou with mee?

BEGGAR: O sir, the ill lucke I have receiued this yeere would make thee verrily weepe.

RICH MAN: Thou hast not had ill lucke, but thou wilt waste thy time in drynkyng and in idlenesse.

BEGGAR: Nay sir, bee gentle with mee. Couldst thou not spare me ten pence, for a cuppe of tea?

RICH MAN: For every halfepence of my money have I worked. If I shoulde dole out charitee to thee, thou wilt spend it on wine onely.

Etc., etc. You could carry on with this conversation if you like. This is another quite difficult activity. It's not just a matter of putting a few extra *es* on the ends of words!

Invasions

A Viking longboat

In Chapter 1, we got as far as saying that the Anglo-Saxons brought English to Britain with them when they invaded. The Anglo-Saxon invasions happened between AD 450 and 700. That's a long time ago, so it's worth mentioning a few important things that have happened to the language since then.

If you go around invading other countries, you mustn't be surprised when you get invaded yourself, as the Anglo-Saxons soon found out. The Vikings began to attack England in about AD 800, and continued their attacks for a century. The Vikings who came to England were Danish and Norwegian. By the end of their century of invasion, they were settling in large numbers in the north and east of England. The language of the Vikings was Old Norse, which wasn't too different from the Old English of the Anglo-Saxons. The two languages slowly mixed in together in the areas where the Vikings had settled, and there must have been a lot of word-swapping and language-switching. Common English words which the Vikings brought into the language are: *egg, skirt, take, anger, ill* and *law*.

In 1066, as everybody knows, the Normans invaded England. The Normans came from Normandy, in north-west France, and they brought their own kind of French with them. Norman French was a different dialect from Central French, which was spoken round Paris. Central French has developed into the kind of French which is taught to English-speaking pupils and students today.

The Norman conquest had an enormous effect on English. The Duke of Normandy, William the Conqueror, became King of England. He gave the money and the power and the land in England to his followers. French became the 'posh' language in England, the language of the king's court, of the new upper classes. At the same time, Latin was the language of the very powerful church. Most books were written in Latin. Educated people spoke in French, wrote in French or Latin. For 200 years after the Norman conquest, English was looked down on as a rough sort of language, spoken by the mass of the common people.

This didn't go on for ever. If it had, we would be writing this book in French or Latin. From about 1250 onwards, English began slowly to fight back against French. It took 150 years for English to win the battle completely, but in the end it did. The Normans had been in England a long time now; they began to feel more English than French. At the beginning of the thirteenth century, the King of France captured Normandy from King John of England. The main connection between Normandy and England was broken. One after the other, the schools, the law courts and Parliament went over to using English. Authors more and more wrote their books in English.

But it wasn't the same English as before 1066. An enormous number of French words came into the language, and have stayed in English ever since. Also, the grammar of the language, the way words are arranged so that they make sense, changed a lot. Some of the French words which came into English at this time are: *people, garden, hour, nature, colour, music, prayer, pork* and *beef*.

The Norman conquest was the last time English was changed by force. It took 300 years for French to work its way right into

English, and in the later part of that time most of the French words were coming from the Central French dialect of Paris, not from Norman French. But if William the Conqueror had lost the Battle of Hastings in 1066, and the Normans had been driven back across the English channel, English today would be very different from what it is.

When we were talking in the last chapter about Cockney and Standard English, we said that Standard English grew out of the East Midlands dialect of English. In the middle ages—from the Norman Conquest until about 1500—there were five main dialects of English, as you can see on the map. There were differences within each of these dialects, as well.

Dialects of English in the Middle Ages

62

Printing

Printing was a very important invention. William Caxton set up his printing press in London in 1476. From that date onwards, written words began to spread at a faster rate than ever before. They have never stopped. Because London is the capital of England, because printed books came mainly from London, the dialect of the educated people of London more and more came to be accepted as normal for writing. London had the power and the money. London had the law courts. Oxford and Cambridge, the two universities, were in the East Midlands dialect area. For all these reasons, the dialect which we now call Standard English became more and more important.

Invention and borrowing

We shall just mention one or two other big changes which have happened to English. One is to do with knowledge. If you find out new things, if you get new knowledge, you need new words to carry that knowledge in. Many of the words we use today have been invented in the last 500 years to deal with new discoveries and ideas. Here are some examples: *nylon, electricity, atom, television, smallpox, thermometer, oxygen.*

Many words which have a common meaning today used to have a different meaning which has almost been forgotten: *plastic* used to mean *something which can be moulded or shaped, peculiar* used to mean *belonging to someone in particular, vulgar* used to mean *to do with ordinary people.*

Some common things in modern life have been named after the person who invented or discovered them: the Earl of *Sandwich* liked eating his meat between slices of bread so he didn't have to leave the card-table, we have 12-*volt* batteries because of an Italian scientist named Volta, and *guillotines* because of a Dr

Guillotin who in 1790 invented a machine for chopping off heads (he used to practise on sheep).

Guillotine is of course a word borrowed from French. English has borrowed many, many words from many languages. You might be quite surprised to know where some of them come from:

From Persian	*From Dutch*	*From Italian*
bazaar	skipper	studio
caravan	schooner	replica
pyjama	yacht	confetti
jackal	dock	balcony
divan	hull	bandit

From Arabic	*From Malay*	*From German*
coffee	bamboo	paraffin
alcohol	ketchup	quartz
algebra	caddy	waltz
sherbet	gong	blitz
magazine	junk	kindergarten

From Nahuatl (the most important Indian language in Mexico)
chocolate
tomato
ranch
coyote
avocado

From Hindi
bungalow
thug
dungarees
punch
cot.

Start your own word-lists under these headings:
1) New scientific words
2) Words which have changed their meaning; what was the old meaning, what is the meaning today?
3) *Sandwich* words—named after a person
4) Words borrowed from other languages.
If you keep these lists in your notebook or folder, you can add to them whenever you come across new examples.

The spread of English

In 1982, about 300 million people across the world speak English as their mother-tongue; it is the language they learn as babies. Millions more people use English as a second, or third, language. In 1066, when Duke William of Normandy arrived in England, the total number of English speakers was about 1½ million, and they all lived in England. So we can see that an important change has happened in the number of people who speak English, and in the places where they speak it. English is now the main language spoken in England, Scotland, Wales, Ireland, United States, Canada, Australia, New Zealand, Jamaica, Trinidad, Barbados, Grenada, Guyana, several more small islands in the Caribbean, and a string of other small places around the world. However, in every one of those places other languages are spoken as well. English didn't get to be so popular by magic, nor because it is somehow better than other languages. It isn't. English is very popular all over the world for reasons to do with history, and to do with power. We shall look at some of these reasons in Chapter 5.

Within English we can find countless varieties; dialects, accents, styles, varieties caused by when you live, where you live, who you are, what you know. We've looked at a few of these varieties in the last two chapters, and we'd like to finish by repeating that *varieties are good*, we ought to be happy that they're there, and the future of English as a beautiful and valuable language depends on them.

Conversations A to F, from oldest to most modern

1) Conversation D is from the *Colloquy* (which means *conversation*) by Aelfric, abbot of Eynsham, written in Latin with an English translation about the year 1000. Here is a modern version:

PUPIL: We children beg you, teacher, to teach us to speak correctly, because we are ignorant and we speak corruptly.

MASTER: What do you want to say?

PUPIL: What do we care what we say, as long as it is correct and proper speech, not trivial or worthless?

MASTER: Are you willing to be beaten in the course of your learning?

PUPIL: We would rather be beaten for the sake of learning than not know anything; but we know that you are kind, and will not give us beatings unless we force you to.

(The letter þ is called a *thorn*. It stood for the sound we make today by the letters *th*.)

2) Conversation F is from *Troilus and Criseyde* by Geoffrey Chaucer. Chaucer finished writing this long poem about 1385. Here is a version in prose:

Pandarus said, 'Madam, God bless you, your friends, and that fine book you're reading!' 'Welcome, uncle!' said Criseyde. She got up, quickly took him by the hand, and said, 'I dreamt of you three times last night. I hope it's a good sign!' Then she sat him down on the bench next to her. 'Yes, niece,' said Pandarus, 'if it's God will, you'll have better luck all this year. But I am sorry I have stopped you reading the book which you like so much. What does it say, for God's sake? Tell me! Is it about love? Maybe you can teach me something useful!' Criseyde said, 'Uncle, your mistress isn't here now!'

(Pandarus is in love with a lady, but the affair isn't going very well.)

3) Conversation B is from *Le Morte Darthur* (*The Death of Arthur*) by Sir Thomas Malory, written in 1469.

'Now put me into the barge,' said the king, and Sir Bedevere put him in gently. And three queens received him there with great mourning, and they sat down, and King Arthur laid his head in one of their laps. That queen said, 'Ah, dear brother! Why have you stayed away from me so long? Alas, this wound on your head has caught too much cold.' So they rowed away from the land, and Sir Bedevere saw all the ladies parting from him. Then he cried, 'Ah, my lord Arthur! What will become of me now you are going and leaving me here alone among my enemies?' 'Comfort yourself,' said the king, 'and do the best you can; for I am not worth trusting in any more. I am going to the Valley of Avilion, to heal my severe wound. If you never hear of me again, pray for my soul.' But the queens and ladies carried on weeping and wailing, so that it was heartbreaking to hear.

4) Conversation C is from *The Winter's Tale* by William Shakespeare, written about 1611. It doesn't really need a translation, but perhaps these words and phrases could be explained:

loathsomenesse—revoltingness
stripes—wounds
apparrell—clothing
footman—man on foot, pedestrian
it hath seene very hot service—it has been very heavily used
softly—gently
a charitable office—a kind deed.

5) Conversation A is from *The Pickwick Papers* by Charles Dickens, published in 1837.

6) Conversation E is from *Brighton Rock* by Graham Greene, published in 1938.

5

Language, Power and People on the Move

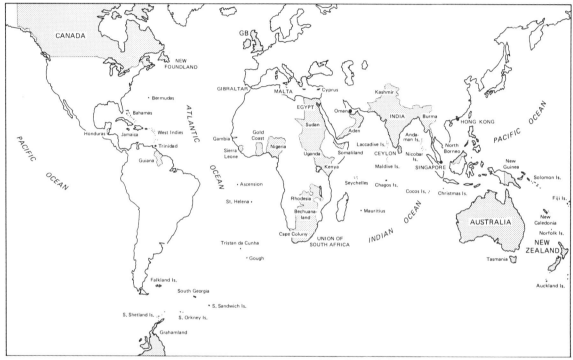

The British Empire at the height of its power

English has travelled all over the world because English-speaking people have taken it with them. This means we'd better ask ourselves the question: why did English-speaking people travel all over the world? That question has many answers. Millions of people were unhappy with life in Britain. They suffered hunger, persecution, unemployment or homelessness. They left Britain hoping for a better life elsewhere. They have been doing that for the last 350 years, at least. Other people travelled the world because they had no choice. They were transported as a punishment. Most important of all, the English language spread across the world because some English-speaking people were interested in power, in wealth and in land. A hundred years ago the British had the biggest empire the world had ever seen. There's hardly any of it left now. But the reason English is such an important world language is mainly to do with that empire.

Now, this is a very big subject, one which you could write a whole book about. All we're going to do is give some examples of the spread of English, to illustrate what we've just said. We'll start close to home, in Britain itself.

English and Welsh

We mentioned the Anglo-Saxons in Chapter 1 and again in Chapter 4. Before they arrived from northern Germany, most of the people in Britain spoke a language which we'll call ancient British. That language, believe it or not, is Welsh, though of course it has changed tremendously in 1500 years. In fact, *Welsh* was an Anglo-Saxon word meaning *foreigner*, which tells us something about the Anglo-Saxons' attitude to the British. Even though the Anglo-Saxons conquered the British, the British (or Welsh) language remained very important in Britain. Up until the 1500s you could find Welsh spoken in large parts of England, and the south of Scotland, as well as in Wales itself. Conquering people is one thing; it's not so easy to kill their language. In the year 1536, in the reign of Henry VIII, an *Act of Union of England and Wales* became law. This Act officially joined the two countries together, and one of the things it had to say was:

> No person or persons that use the Welsh speech or language shall have or enjoy any Manner Office or Fees within this realm of England Wales or other the King's Dominion, upon pain of forfeiting the same Offices or Fees, unless he or they use and exercise the English Speech or Language.

In simple terms, no Welsh was to be spoken by anyone who had power or authority of any kind. So Welsh became the language of the poorer people, and the area where it was spoken grew smaller. Land-owners and government officials in Wales spoke English, and looked down on Welsh speakers as ignorant. All documents were written in English. Welsh was under attack.

The Bible was translated into Welsh in 1588, and this is one important reason why the language has not died out altogether. The battle between the two languages went on, with English slowly winning all the time. In the middle of the nineteenth century, Welsh children who spoke their language is school were punished. They had a piece of wood, called the *Welsh not*, hung round their necks, and they were beaten and fined. In 1870 a law was passed which made it compulsory for all children to go to school, but it said nothing about Welsh in Welsh schools. Education was to be in English.

This century, Welsh has begun to fight back against English. Welsh is used in many schools in Wales now. Sometimes it is taught as a subject, sometimes it is the language in which other subjects are taught. Very few people in Wales want to drive out English completely; that would be unrealistic. But many people feel that Welsh and English should be equally important. In 1975, English and Welsh were given equal importance in the Welsh lawcourts. To get a job in Wales as a teacher, librarian or government official, it is now often necessary to be able to speak Welsh.

One of the best-known battles between Welsh and English was about road-signs. In 1962, the Welsh Language Society was formed. Members of the society thought it was wrong that road-signs in Wales should only be in English. So they began to saw down or paint over road-signs where only the English name of a place was given, or where the Welsh word was spelt in an English way. The seaside town of Conwy, on the north coast of Wales, was signposted *Conway*, the English spelling. The Welsh Language Society went round painting out the *a* on the signposts. One of their members, Dafydd Iwan, was taken to court for doing this, but he won his case, and now the signposts say *Conwy*. Road-signs in Wales must now be in Welsh, or in both languages.

Members of the Welsh Language Society have been in trouble with the law many times. At one case, a judge said this to seven members who had been removing and destroying English road-signs: 'There is no doubt that each of you have some fine qualities. None of you lack courage. You are all prepared to make sacrifices for what you believe. One or two of you have the highest quality of all, a basic humility.' Another time, when members of the Society had been damaging equipment at the Granada Television Centre in Manchester, the judge said: 'I want it understood that every court is loath to sentence men who, in their sincere beliefs, commit offences. But I have to sentence you for the offences concerning the destruction of valuable property.'

Do you think that the Welsh Language Society were right to do what they did? How far should people go in defending their beliefs or their language? Talk about these questions in a pair or a group.

The fightback by Welsh in this century may have come too late. Some people feel that four centuries of persecution, from Henry VIII's time onwards, will prove fatal, and the language will die. Other people disagree very strongly; they say the language will survive, and they are determined to see that it does.

Scots Gaelic and Irish

The battle between English and Welsh is one example of a struggle between languages. There have been similar battles over the Gaelic spoken in the highlands of Scotland and in the Hebrides, and over the Irish language. Scots Gaelic and Irish have suffered even more than Welsh. Both languages were banned by the English government in the eighteenth century. That didn't work, of course. You can't *ban* a language. In Scotland and Ireland, people went on speaking their language.

EJECTMENT OF IRISH PEASANTS.
Illustrated London News, 1848.

But children in the schools 100 years ago had the same sort of treatment as Welsh children. As well as that, many Scots Gaelic and Irish speakers had their land taken from them by the English government, or they were driven off land which they rented when the landowners wanted more profitable methods of farming. In Ireland in 1845, 1846 and 1847 there was a famine when the potato crop went rotten with the blight. Thousands and thousands of people starved to death.

Emigration

Many Irish and Scottish people left their country for ever. They went across the sea to America, Canada, Australia or New Zealand, or they went to cities like London, Manchester, Liverpool or Glasgow, looking for work and a new life.

In those places, they found they needed to speak English. Many of them spoke English already; they had been forced to. Others learnt it quickly. Their children grew up speaking American or Australian or Liverpool English. English is the language of their grandchildren and great-grandchildren, although you can still find people around the world who speak Scots Gaelic and Irish too.

It was not only Scottish, Irish or Welsh people who left Britain and Ireland for other parts of the world. Many English people did the same thing for some of the same reasons. New methods of farming meant that farmers didn't need so many labourers. When there were bad harvests, food became expensive and hard to get. A hundred and fifty years ago, the slums of English cities were terrible places to live. Wages were low in many jobs, and there were very few trade unions to bargain for better pay and conditions. Unemployment could mean starvation or the workhouse. Millions of English people, throughout the nineteenth century, decide to risk the unknown. They sailed away to the colonies, or to the United States (which had once been a British colony).

In the 1830s, 50,000 people left Britain and Ireland every year. Each year of 1847, 1848 and 1849, a quarter of a million emigrated as a result of the potato famine. During the 1850s, the number was 120,000 per year. In the 1870s, 100,000 people from England alone emigrated each year. They took their language with them, of course. English travelled far and wide.

At the start of the chapter, we said that some people were transported abroad as a punishment. From the early 1600s onwards, they were sent to America. But after America became independent in 1776, the British government started convict settlements in Australia and Tasmania. The settlement at Botany Bay, near Sydney in Australia, took prisoners between 1786 and 1853. Some prisoners were real criminals like murderers and violent robbers. Other people were transported for small offences, like poaching. In 1834, some farm labourers from Tolpuddle in Dorset were transported because they had formed a trade union. Here are two songs about being sent to Botany Bay:

Botany Bay

Come all young men of learning and a
 warning take by me,
I would have you quit night walking and
 shun bad company;

I would have you quit night walking, or else
 you'll rue the day,
You'll rue your transportation, lads, when
 you're bound for
 Botany Bay.

I was brought up in London Town at a place
 I know full well,
Brought up by honest parents, for the truth
 to you I'll tell;
Brought up by honest parents and reared
 most tenderly,
Till I became a roving blade, which proved
 my destiny.

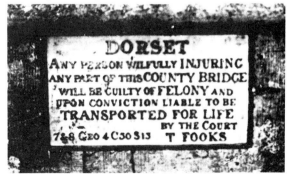

DORSET
ANY PERSON WILFULLY INJURING
ANY PART OF THIS COUNTY BRIDGE
WILL BE GUILTY OF FELONY AND
UPON CONVICTION LIABLE TO BE
TRANSPORTED FOR LIFE
BY THE COURT
7&8 GEO 4 C30 S13   T FOOKS

A convict settlement

My character soon was taken and I was sent
to jail;
My friends they tried to clear me but
nothing could prevail.
At the Old Bailey Sessions the judge to me
did say,
'The jury's found you guilty lad, you must
go to Botany Bay.'

To see my agèd father dear as he stood at
the bar,
Likewise my tender mother, her old grey
locks to tear;
In tearing of her old grey locks, these words
to me did say,
'Oh son, oh son, what have you done, that
you're going to Botany Bay?'

It was on the twenty-eighth of May, from
England we did steer;
And all things being made safe on board we
sailed down the river clear;
And every ship that we passed by, we heard
the sailors say,
'There goes a ship of clever hands, and
they're bound for Botany Bay.'

There is a girl in Manchester, a girl I know
full well;
And if ever I get my liberty, along with her
I'll dwell.
Oh, then I mean to marry her and no more
go astray;
I'll shun all evil company, bid adieu to
Botany Bay.

Jim Jones

Oh listen for a moment, lads, and hear me
tell my tale,
How o'er the sea from England's shore I
was compelled to sail.
The jury says, 'He's guilty, sir,' and says
the judge, says he,
'For life, Jim Jones, I'm sending you across
the stormy sea.

'And take a tip before you ship to join the
iron gang,
Don't get too gay at Botany Bay or else
you'll surely hang;
Or else you'll surely hang,' he says, says he,
'and after that, Jim Jones,
It's high upon the gallows tree the crows
will pick your bones.

'You'll have no time for mischief, then,
remember what I say;
They'll flog the poaching out of you when
you get to Botany Bay.'
The waves were high upon the sea, the winds
blew up in gales;
I'd rather be drowned in misery than go to
New South Wales.

The winds blew high upon the sea and
pirates came along,
But soldiers on our convict ship were full
five hundred strong;
They opened fire and somehow drove that
pirate ship away,

I'd rather have joined that pirate ship than
  come to Botany Bay.

For day and night the irons clang, and, like
  poor galley slaves,
We toil and moil and when we die must fill
  dishonoured graves;
But by and by I'll break my chains, into the
  bush I'll go,
And join the brave bushrangers there, Jack
  Donahue and Co.

And some dark night when everything is
  silent in the town,
I'll kill the tyrants one and all and shoot the
  floggers down;
I'll give the law a little shock—remember
  what I say;
They'll yet regret they sent Jim Jones in
  chains to Botany Bay.

> iron gang—gang of convicts, who worked
>   chained together.
> Jack Donahue—a famous ex-convict who
>   escaped to the bush. Men who did this
>   were called *bushrangers*.

Look closely at the ballads to see what
information they give us about
transportation. What is the difference in
attitude between the two singers? Look at
the shape of the ballads; the kind of verse
they use, the rhymes and repetitions. Then
try a piece of writing called *Two
Transportation Ballads*.

Exploration The early Portuguese voyages

So far, we have thought about people who
were forced to move, forced to change,
people who had very little power
themselves. Alongside these people, there
were English-speaking people with a great
deal of power, and they also helped to
make English a world language. To
illustrate this, let us go to one part of the
world in particular: west Africa.

The first European people to sail down
the coast of west Africa were the
Portuguese. Portugal is the nearest
European country to west Africa, and the
Portuguese were great sailors and
navigators. As well as that, they were
interested in gold, and in other kinds of
wealth which they hoped to find in Africa.
From 1460 onwards, they began to set up
forts and bases, and to trade with the
African people. Sadly, very few of them
were content to trade fairly with the
Africans. They wanted to get rich quick,
and they used tricks, lies, swords and
gunpowder to help them.

The first English people did not reach
west Africa until the next century. Their
serious trading only began in the century
after that, the early 1600s. They treated
the Africans as the Portuguese did, often
using trickery and violence. The question
we are interested in here is: how did
Africans and English talk to each other?

The English traders used to send young
African men back to England, where they
would live for a while and learn English.
Then they would return to Africa, and
become interpreters between their people
and the English. That's one answer. The
second answer is a bit more complicated to
explain. Many of the people living on the
west coast of Africa in the 1600s were
good at languages. Hundreds of languages
were spoken around that area, so it was
quite common to know one or two
languages besides your mother-tongue.
This was especially true for people who
were leaders, who had to travel and do
business. So when English people
appeared for the first time, Africans began
to pick up English words and use them for

73

Elmina, the first settlement on the Gold Coast, founded by the Portuguese in 1541

The British fort at Cape Coast Castle about 1670

trading and discussion. They were good at swapping languages. They were used to it. They developed simple trading languages which used a lot of English words together with some words from their own languages, and usually arranged the words according to the grammar of their mother-tongue. These trading languages, called *pidgins*, are still very important in west Africa, and are used in Nigeria, Ghana, Sierra Leone, Gambia and other countries. They are used between an African person and an English-speaking person, and also when African people, who speak different languages, want to communicate.

Here is a poem written in Krio, the pidgin language of Sierra Leone. Krio is the mother-tongue of many people in Sierra Leone, and is used by others as a second language. The poem is called *Dinner Time*, and is by Gladys Hayford. Try reading it to yourself first, and then check the words you don't understand, in the standard English translation.

Dinner Time

Jen go pul di fufu, Ayo ton di pot,
Bobo yu go was den plet, mek di sup de ot.

Maraya no kam bak yet? Lod da pikin slo!
A jes sen am fo go bai res, from lon tem we i go?

Soni de ple bol na trit. I tink se in de wet
Fo mek a kol am? A no ful, mi bisin if i let?

Tunu, tel yu sisi se if i no go tap
Fo nak da piano bom, bom, bom, en trai kam dong kam chop?

U ambog mi no go get wan gren drai fish sef.
Jen yu pas di koba dish we de pantap da shelf.

Ol man fo go was den pan! ol man was den spun
I luk lek una ol no wan go skul dis aftanun.

Jen, Bobo, Tunu, Maraya, Sisi, Soni, Swit,
Se yu gres en tek yu plet, tel tenki en go it.

74

Standard English translation

Jane go serve the foofoo, Ayo stir the pot,
Bobo go and wash the plates while the soup
  gets hot.
Has Maria not come back yet? Lord, how
  slow that child is!
I only sent her to buy some rice; what a long
  time she's been gone!
Sonny is playing ball in the street. Does he
  think he is waiting
For me to call him? I'm no fool, what do I
  care if he is late?
Tunu, ask your sister if she will never stop
Banging that piano bom, bom, bom and
  bring herself down to eat?
Anyone who bothers me will not get even a
  shred of stockfish.
Jane you hand me the covered dish which is
  standing on the shelf.
Let each one of you go and wash his plate!
  each one wash his spoon.
It looks as if you all do not wish to go to
  school this afternoon!
Jane, Bobo, Tunu, Maria, Sisi, Sonny,
  Sweet,
Say your grace and take your plate, say
  thanks, go on and eat.

  foofoo—a dish made out of yams,
    plantains or cassavas

A language born in slavery

In Chapter 3 we saw several examples of Jamaican creole. Jamaican creole, the language of Jamaica, has its roots in the west African pidgins, and so do other languages in the Caribbean. In about 1630, the British began their slave trade. Over the next 200 years, they shipped millions of Africans across the Atlantic Ocean, and forced them to work on sugar, tobacco and cotton plantations. These plantations were on islands in the Caribbean which the British had grabbed, and also on the fertile plains of the southern colonies of America.

Two sides of slavery—capture and revolt

75

TO BE SOLD, on board the

Ship *Bance-Island*, on tuesday the 6th of *May* next, at *Ashley-Ferry*; a choice cargo of about 250 fine healthy

NEGROES,

just arrived from the Windward & Rice Coast. —The utmost care has already been taken, and shall be continued, to keep them free from the least danger of being infected with the SMALL-POX, no boat having been on board, and all other communication with people from *Charles-Town* prevented.

Austin, Laurens, & Appleby.

N. B. Full one Half of the above Negroes have had the SMALL-POX in their own Country..

British slave traders and plantation owners were afraid that the Africans might rebel against this treatment. (They were right to be afraid. There were many rebellions.) So when groups of Africans were taken out of the slave ships, those who spoke the same language were split up and sent to different plantations, or put back on other ships and sent to different islands. Africans were banned from using their own language. They were told that they must speak English. Those who disobeyed were punished, by flogging or other methods.

What would you do if you were forbidden to speak your language? You might say, 'I'd learn another one.' You might say, 'I'd disobey the order.' Africans did both these things. Some of them carried on using their language when they could, and risked punishment. Some tried to escape from slavery, and ran away to the wild, mountainous parts of the islands, where they spoke their own language in freedom. But we have to remember that many slaves, working together on the same plantation, spoke different languages anyway. Escaping from the plantation was dangerous. If they were caught they were likely to be put to death. They did the same thing as other Africans had done back in Africa. A few of them already knew some pidgin English from before the terrible experience of the slave ship. They learnt English words, and mixed them with words from their own languages. Mostly, they used the grammar systems of the most important west African languages. (Remember, grammar means the way words are arranged so that they make sense.) They also threw in a few words from Spanish, Portuguese and French. It was like a stewing pot of language. They didn't do it all at once, but they did it in an amazingly short time. By the end of the 1600s, all over the Caribbean, these new languages were springing up. Soon, babies were born who heard the new language around them more than the old African languages. These babies learnt the new language as their mother-tongue. The new languages came to be known as creoles, and you can look back to Chapter 3 to see one of those creoles, Jamaican, in use 300 years later.

The Jamaican literature in Chapter 3 was written by school pupils in London. Here is a poem by Louise Bennett, a Jamaican writer well-known in the Caribbean and in Britain. The poem is called *Colonization in Reverse*. It completes a triangle which we have sketched in this chapter. It describes the migration of many Jamaican people to England, in the 1950s. Remember that there were migrations from many other parts of the Caribbean, to England, at the same time.

Louise Bennett

Colonization in Reverse

Wat a joyful news, Miss Mattie,
I feel like me heart gwine burs'
Jamaica people colonizin
Englan in reverse.

By de hundred, by de t'ousan
From country and from town,
By de ship-load, by de plane-load
Jamaica is Englan boun.

Dem a-pour out o'Jamaica,
Everybody future plan
Is fe get a big-time job
An settle in de mother lan.

What a islan! What a people!
Man an woman, old an young
Jusa pack dem bag an baggage
An tun history upside dung!

Some people don't like travel,
But fe show dem loyalty
Dem all a-open up cheap-fare-
To-Englan agency.

An week by week dem shippin off
Dem countryman like fire,
Fe immigrate an populate
De seat o' de Empire.

Oonoo see how life is funny,
Oonoo see de tunabout,
Jamaica live fe box bread
Outa English people mout'.

For wen dem catch a Englan,
An start play dem different role,
Some will settle down to work
And some will settle fe de dole.

Jane say de dole is not too bad
Because dey payin' she
Two pounds a week fe seek a job
Dat suit her dignity.

Me say Jane will never find work
At the rate how she dah-look,
For all day she stay pon Aunt Fan couch
An read love-story book.

Wat a devilment a Englan!
Dem face war an brave de worse,
But I'm wonderin' how dem gwine stan'
Colonizin' in reverse.

> fe—*to*, except in verse eight, where it
>   means *for*
> oonoo—you
> catch a Englan—settle in England

Ask yourself these questions about
Colonization in Reverse;
1) How does the poem *complete a triangle*?
2) What is the meaning of the title? Have people from the Caribbean really colonized England since the 1950s?
3) The speaker of the poem and the writer of the poem are not the same person. Does the poet intend us to agree with what the speaker says?
4) The speaker of the poem is talking to her friend, Miss Mattie. Does the poet keep the style of a chatty conversation, all the way through?

Empire

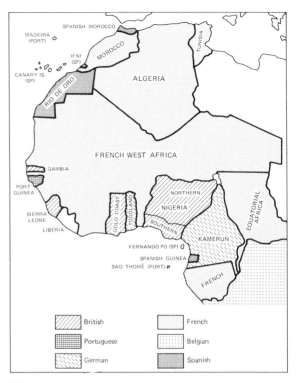

West Africa under empire—1914

Independent West Africa

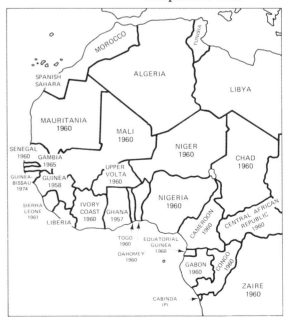

Let us return to west Africa. If you go to Nigeria or Ghana today, you will meet plenty of English, spoken and written. Some of that English will be one of the pidgins we have already mentioned. But you will also find Standard English, used in schools, colleges, businesses and government. This may seem strange when very few Nigerian or Ghanaian people speak English as their mother-tongue. As babies, they learn one of the African languages. In Nigeria, it might be Hausa, Yoruba or Ibo; in Ghana, it might be Twi, Fanti or Ewe. English is an important language in these countries because it is the *official* language. We will have to look back into history to see why this is so.

The first contact between English and west African people, as we have seen, was for trading. This soon developed into the horrors of the slave trade, and for nearly 200 years the British used Africa as an endless source of slave labour. So did other European countries. But in 1807 the British parliament abolished slavery. There had been many revolts by the slaves themselves. Wealthy English people were now not so interested in growing sugar in the Caribbean; there were other things to make profit from, and it was tiresome and expensive to keep crushing the slave revolts. Also, some important people in Britain thought slavery was wicked, and said so loudly. When the slave trade stopped, business people and politicians decided that, instead of making wealth *out of* Africa, they would see what wealth could be made *in* Africa. Throughout the nineteenth century, the European countries carved up Africa like a roast chicken. They sent in their armies to put down any resistance they met. The technique they preferred was to get the leaders of the African peoples to sign away their independence; in return for this, the Europeans offered 'protection'. If this technique failed, guns and soldiers were used. Britain had control of big chunks of Africa, including Nigeria and the Gold Coast (the old name for Ghana).

Naturally, the British governors, administrators, soldiers and business people spoke English. Missionaries came, and set up schools, medical stations and churches. Their teaching and preaching was mainly in English. At first, they used interpreters. They expected the children who came to their schools to learn English as quickly as possible. Some missionaries, it is true, did learn the African languages, and began to translate parts of the Bible.

MISSIONARY WORK IN AFRICA.

Here is an extract from *Things Fall Apart*, a novel by Chinua Achebe. Achebe is Nigeria's best-known novelist. *Things Fall Apart* is set in Nigeria at the end of the nineteenth century. This extract tells us something about missionaries, about religion, and about language too.

The arrival of the missionaries had caused a considerable stir in the village of Mbanta. There were six of them and one was a white man. Every man and woman came out to see the white man. Stories about these strange men had grown since one of them had been killed in Abame and his iron horse tied to the sacred silk-cotton tree. And so everybody came to see the white man. It was the time of year when everybody was at home. The harvest was over.

Chinua Achebe

When they had all gathered, the white man began to speak to them. He spoke through an interpreter who was an Ibo man, though his dialect was different and harsh to the ears of Mbanta. Many people laughed at his dialect and the way he used words strangely. Instead of saying 'myself' he always said 'my buttocks'. But he was a man of commanding presence and the clansmen listened to him. He said he was one of them, as they could see from his colour and his language. The other four black men were also their brothers, although one of them did not speak Ibo. The white man was also their brother because they were all sons of God. And he told them about this new God, the Creator of all the world and all the men and women. He told them that they worshipped false gods, gods of wood and stone. A deep murmur went through the crowd when he said this. He told them that the true God lived on high and that all men when they died went before Him for judgment. Evil men and all the heathen who in their blindness bowed to wood and stone were thrown into a fire that burned like palm-oil. But good men who worshipped the true God lived for ever in his happy kingdom. 'We have been sent by this great God to ask you to leave your wicked ways and false gods and turn to Him so that you can be saved when you die,' he said.

'Your buttocks understand our language,' said someone light-heartedly and the crowd laughed.

'What did he say?' the white man asked his interpreter. But before he could answer, another man asked a question: 'Where is the white man's horse?' he asked. The Ibo evangelists consulted among themselves and decided that the man probably meant bicycle. They told the white man and he smiled benevolently.

'Tell them,' he said, 'that I shall bring many iron horses when we have settled down among them. Some of them will even ride the iron horse themselves.' This was interpreted to them but very few of them heard. They were talking excitedly among themselves because the white man had said he was going to live among them. They had not thought about that.

At this point an old man said he had a question. 'Which is this god of yours,' he asked, 'the goddess of the earth, the god of the sky, Amadiora of the thunderbolt, or what?'

The interpreter spoke to the white man and he immediately gave his answer. 'All the gods you have named are not gods at all. They are gods of deceit who tell you to kill your fellows and destroy innocent children. There is only one true God and He has the earth, the sky, you and me and all of us.'

'If we leave our gods and follow your god,'

asked another man, 'who will protect us from the anger of our neglected gods and ancestors?'

'Your gods are not alive and cannot do you any harm,' replied the white man. 'They are pieces of wood and stone.'

When this was interpreted to the men of Mbanta they broke into derisive laughter. These men must be mad, they said to themselves. How else could they say that Ani and Amadiora were harmless? And Idemili and Ogwugwu too? And some of them began to go away.

Then the missionaries burst into song. It was one of those gay and rollicking tunes of evangelism which had the power of plucking at silent and dusty chords in the heart of an Ibo man. The interpreter explained each verse to the audience, some of whom now stood enthralled. It was a story of brothers who lived in darkness and in fear, ignorant of the love of God. It told of one sheep out on the hills, away from the gates of God and from the tender shepherd's care.

After the singing the interpreter spoke about the Son of God whose name was Jesu Kristi. Okonkwo, who only stayed in the hope that it might come to chasing the men out of the village or whipping them, now said:

'You told us with your own mouth that there was only one god. Now you talk about his son. He must have a wife, then.' The crowd agreed.

'I did not say He had a wife,' said the interpreter, somewhat lamely.

'Your buttocks said he had a son,' said the joker. 'So he must have a wife and all of them must have buttocks.'

The missionary ignored him and went on to talk about the Holy Trinity. At the end of it Okonkwo was fully convinced that the man was mad. He shrugged his shoulders and went away to tap his afternoon palm-wine.

But there was a young lad who had been captivated. His name was Nwoye, Okonkwo's first son. It was not the mad logic of the Trinity that captivated him. He did not understand it. It was the poetry of the new religion, something felt in the marrow. The hymn about brothers who sat in darkness and in fear seemed to answer a vague and persistent question that haunted his young soul . . . . . He felt a relief within as the hymn poured into his parched soul. The words of the hymn were like drops of frozen rain melting on the dry palate of the panting earth. Nwoye's callow mind was greatly puzzled.

Ask yourself these questions about the extract from *Things Fall Apart*:
1) Where does the writing make us think about language, particularly? Make a list of all the places.
2) Where does the writing make us think about religion, particularly? Make a list of all those places.
3) The religion needs the language to explain itself. There are places in the extract where the language doesn't explain the religion very well—the missionaries' religion or the villagers' religion. Can you see where this happens?

Very few children had any education at all until the 1950s, just before Nigeria and Ghana became independent. Since becoming independent countries, Nigeria and Ghana have increased opportunities for education very fast. Nearly all children now go to primary school, and secondary schools, colleges and universities are taking more and more students. After the first two or three years of primary school, education is in English. All jobs which require educational qualifications require English. English is the official language of government and business. It is the language of power.

In Ghana, over 40 languages are spoken by the people. In Nigeria, which has a population of about 70 million, 250 languages are spoken. So English has an important job to do, in providing one language which everyone can use for the official business of the nation. English will play a big part in the future of Nigeria, of

Ghana, and of many other African countries. But we must not forget the reasons why English has become a world language in this way. It didn't happen by accident or by magic. It happened because English-speaking people went to Africa looking for wealth and power—and found it.

Here is a demanding activity which will involve you in some research. Make a world map of English. You'll need to use an atlas, an encyclopaedia, and books on world history and languages. On an outline map of the world, mark the places where English is spoken. Show the differences between places where English is spoken by nearly all the people as a first language, by some of the people as a first language, or is used as a second or official language.

Another empire

It's important to remember that the British were not the only people who went to Africa looking for wealth and power. So did the French, the Germans, the Spanish, the Portuguese, the Italians, the Dutch and the Belgians. France controlled more land in west Africa than any other European country. They called that land *French West Africa*. A railway ran across the territory from Dakar to Niger. In 1947 the Africans who worked the railway went on strike. They demanded the same pay and conditions as railway workers in France.

Sembene Ousmane is a writer and film director who was born in Senegal, which was then part of French West Africa. He wrote a novel, in French, about the strike. The English translation is called *God's Bits of Wood*. In this extract, the African strike leaders and the French railway directors meet to negotiate. Bakayoko, Doudou, Lahbib and Balla are the Africans. Their first language is Ouolof. Isnard, Victor, Edouard, Dejean and Pierre are the Frenchmen. Their only language is French.

Sembene Ousmane

'We will use French for this meeting,' Edouard said, looking at Bakayoko.

'Since we are all Frenchmen,' Victor added, with a mirthless smile.

It was Lahbib who answered. 'Since there is no intermediary language, we will use French.'

But Edouard insisted. 'Do you agree, Monsieur Bakayoko?'

Bakayoko was sitting in the relaxed position which seemed to be his habit, leaning slightly to one side and far back in his chair.

'I am not alone in this strike,' he said, looking at the personnel director, 'but since your ignorance of any of our language is a handicap for you, we will use French as a matter of courtesy. But it is a courtesy that will not last forever.'

They all stared at him. Dejean's face turned purple, and Victor half rose from his chair.

'Be careful what you say—your words may cause you trouble!'

'Monsieur,' Bakayoko said, 'we are here for a discussion among equals, and not to listen to your threats.'

The negotiations had started badly, and now a thick wall of silence seemed to rise up as the men on either side of the table took each other's measure.

It was Dejean, mastering his anger, who broke through it first. 'Very well,' he said.

'Let's get down to this list of grievances.'

'They are not grievances,' Lahbib said. He was too simple a man to amuse himself with a game of words, but he respected them and did not like to see them misused.

Dejean went on as if he had not even heard him. 'Re-evaluation of salaries . . . . .'

'A twenty per cent increase all along the line,' Doudou said automatically and began distributing some sheets of paper to his comrades, although he knew perfectly well that at least half of them did not know how to write.

'Annual paid vacations, pensions, family allowances . . . . .', Dejean continued.

'Payment of back wages, based on the settlement with French railway workers in July 1936; contractual bonus of six thousand francs to the trainmen, at the same rate of interest paid by French trainmen,' Doudou said, spreading a year-old copy of the *Journal Officiel* on the table.

'That's all?' Dejean demanded. 'Don't you think it's a little too much?'

'And you, monsieur?' Bakayoko said. 'Don't you think this thieving has lasted long enough?'

'You are not in charge here!'

'If you look at the list of delegates, you will find my name.'

'I'll warn you just once more—if you go on in this manner I shall adjourn the meeting.'

Doudou leaned toward Lahbib and said in Ouolof, 'It would be better if Bakayoko would be quiet. The red-eared men are going to get angry with him and use it as an excuse to send us all away. They're just waiting for the chance.'

'It's true, Bakayoko,' Balla said. 'Don't answer him again, or they'll break up the meeting.'

Pierre had followed the earlier discussion excitedly, and now, almost without thinking, he demanded, 'What are you saying? I can't understand you.'

'If we are content, we speak French and you understand. If we are not content, you can't understand,' Bella said, summoning up his best French. Pleased with this answer, he looked around the table at his comrades, seeking their approval.

Bakayoko's heavy lips sketched a smile. He leaned back in his chair, took his tobacco pouch from his pocket, and began to fill his pipe.

Use the extract from *God's Bits of Wood* as a starting-point for a piece of drama. This could be:

1) a playscript of your own which involves a meeting, and an important argument about language;
2) an improvised scene about a strike—the two sides bargaining with each other;
3) a playscript or improvisation about any tense, angry situation: a disagreement at home, a quarrel in the street, a confrontation between two groups.

English in America

We have chosen in the last few pages to look closely at Africa—at one part of Africa. There are other places in the world where we could have gone; to India, for instance. English has an important position in the life of modern India, where the 600 million people speak about 150 languages between them. In Africa or in India, English is mainly used as a *second* or *official* language. Of all the countries across the world where English is the *first* language, let us stop and look at one—the United States of America.

A small American farm in the 1920s

The USA has more English speakers than any other country. About 200 million people speak it as their first language. It is the national language of the country, so that most people there whose first language is, say, Spanish, German, Italian or Polish, learn English too. The USA has

immense power and influence in the world, which is another reason for the international importance of English.

In the early 1600s, the British, French and Spanish governments were arguing over who should control the new lands which had been found across the ocean. The British had the best of the argument, and they set up colonies all along the east and south coasts of America. People went to live in the colonies for various reasons. Most of those reasons we've already mentioned in this chapter, but let us quickly go over them again. Some people emigrated because they suffered in England for their religious beliefs; for instance, Quakers and Roman Catholics. Some were people who had been turned off the land where they worked. Some were transported to the new colonies as a punishment. Some were unemployed and desperate. Some were enterprising young men and women who wanted the challenge of a new kind of life, and hoped to prosper in America. The British government encouraged them by setting up companies to invest money in the colonies.

Here's a cheerful but ignorant ballad about the joys of settling in America.

The Buffalo

Come all you young fellows that have a mind
  to range
Into some foreign country, your station for
  to change;
Into some foreign country away from home
  to go,
We'll lay down on the banks of the pleasant
  Ohio,
We'll wander through the wild woods and
  we'll chase the buffalo.

There are fishes in the river that are fitting
  for our use,
And high and lofty sugar canes that yield us
  pleasant juice,
All sorts of game, my boys, besides the buck
  and doe,
We'll lay down on the banks of the pleasant
  Ohio,
We'll wander through the wild woods and
  we'll chase the buffalo.

Come all you young maidens, come spin us
up some yarn,
To make us some new clothing to keep
ourselves full warm;
For you can card and spin, my girls, and we
can reap and mow,
We'll lay down on the banks of the pleasant
Ohio,
We'll wander through the wild woods and
we'll chase the buffalo.

Supposing these wild Indians by chance
should come us near,
We will unite together our hearts all free
from care;
We will march down into the town, my boys,
and give the fatal blow,
We'll lay down on the banks of the pleasant
Ohio,
We'll wander through the wild woods and
we'll chase the buffalo.

The Buffalo doesn't give a very realistic
picture of what life would be like for
people going to America. What
differences would there be between the
ballad's version, and reality? What does
the singer mean by *your station for to
change*? What about the singer's view
of buffalo, of Indians, or of young
maidens?

So began the great flow of people into
America. As well as British and Irish
people, Germans, Dutch, French, Swiss
and Scandinavians arrived. African people
came too, by force, as we have seen, to the
plantations of the south. English was the
main language in these British-owned
colonies. In 1776, after bitter struggle and
a war, America became independent.
Throughout the nineteenth century,
people continued to pour into the country.
In the 1890s, and in the early part of this
century, they began to come more from
the south and east of Europe, from Italy,
Greece, Poland, Russia, Austria or
Hungary. Many Jewish people fled from
persecution in eastern Europe and Russia.
Italians and Greeks fled from desperate
poverty in their countries. America had a
reputation for being free and rich. There
was plenty of space there. There were
opportunities.

New York harbour, 1900

We can imagine, say, a small group of
Italians sailing into New York harbour for
the first time. The year is 1900. They have
all their belongings and all their money
with them. They have some relations
already in America, and they have a letter
introducing them to other Italians who,
they hope, may be able to find work for
them. They are ready to work. They hope
that their saved money will be enough to
see them through until they get jobs. They

know that one of the first things they must do is learn some English. In weeks, months and years that follow, they do learn English. Some learn it better than others. They learn it simply by hearing it spoken, by working out what words mean, by trying to speak it themselves, by seeing it on advertisements, news-stands, shop-signs. Usually, the more they have to speak English, the better they learn it. They begin to have children. Those children grow up with two languages. Their first language is still Italian. It is spoken at home, they learn it as babies. But playing in the street, and later going to school, English becomes more important. By the time these children have grown up, got jobs, had children of their own, English may have become the first language.

Look back to Chapter 2, and the story of Grace and Virginia. Remember the mixture of languages which went into the language they invented.

What do we mean by *English*, as used in America? People in Britain know what they mean by an *American accent*, or they think they do. If you go to America, you will find lots of American accents. American people can tell quickly whether someone comes from the south, or from California, or from New York. In Britain, American accents are heard all the time, mainly through films and television. But, as we said in Chapter 3, accent is only one part of language. There are differences of vocabulary between American and British English:

American	British
sidewalk	pavement
elevator	lift
fall	autumn
pants	trousers

There are also differences of spelling:

American	British
center	centre
flavor	flavour
program	programme
mommy	mummy

And there are differences of grammar and word use:

American	British
She dove into the pool	She dived into the pool
From September through February	From September until February
He's real nice	He's really nice
I've gotten a cold	I've got a cold

Some words are pronounced differently, like *aluminium, schedule* and *leisure*.

Perhaps the most important differences between American and British English are the ones which show the differences between American and British life. You might *walk four blocks* in New York, but you wouldn't do it in Manchester because Manchester isn't laid out in blocks. In America you'll *go through high school*; in Britain you *go to secondary school*. If you ask for *salf beef on rye* in Chicago, they know you want a certain kind of sandwich. You'll be very lucky to get one of those in Britain, and we know that *salt beef on rye* 'sounds American'.

Make your own lists of differences between American and British English. Use the examples we've given as starters, if you like. Or, instead of lists, try a piece of writing called *American and British English*.

American language has had a big effect on English in Britain. This has a lot to do with the American films, television programmes, magazines and books in Britain.

Do a survey of one week's television, using *Radio Times*, or *TV Times*, or preferably both. Work out how many of the programmes come from America. You can organize your survey in various ways. For instance, which of the channels shows the most American programmes, and which the fewest? Group all the programmes on television into types: feature films, documentaries, half-hour comedy series, police programmes, sports programmes, news programmes. Which of these groups uses American programmes the most? Take one American programme, watch it on television, and then describe it in detail. Or compare, say, an American police programme with a British one. Try to get behind the story, and talk or write about the differences between Britain and America which the programmes show.

American detective novels are very popular in Britain. Here is an extract from one of the best-known of them, *Farewell my Lovely*, by Raymond Chandler.

It was a warm day, almost the end of March, and I stood outside the barber shop looking up at the jutting neon sign of a second floor dine and dice emporium called Florian's. A man was looking up at the sign too. He was looking up at the dusty windows with a sort of ecstatic fixity of expression, like a hunky immigrant catching his first sight of the Statue of Liberty. He was a big man but not more than six feet five inches tall and not wider than a beer truck. He was about ten feet away from me. His arms hung loose at his sides and a forgotten cigar smoked between his enormous fingers.

Slim quiet negroes passed up and down the street and stared at him with darting side glances. He was worth looking at. He wore a shaggy borsalino hat, a rough grey sports coat with white golf balls on it for buttons, a brown shirt, a yellow tie, pleated grey flannel slacks and alligator shoes with white explosions on the toes. From his outer breast pocket cascaded a show handkerchief of the same brilliant yellow as his tie. There were a couple of coloured feathers tucked into the band of his hat, but he didn't really need them. Even on Central Avenue, not the quietest dressed street in the world, he looked about as inconspicuous as a tarantula on a slice of angel food.

His skin was pale and he needed a shave. He would always need a shave. He had curly black hair and heavy eyebrows that almost met over his thick nose. His ears were small and neat for a man of that size and his eyes had a shine close to tears that grey eyes often seem to have. He stood like a statue, and after a long time he smiled.

He moved slowly across the sidewalk to the double swinging doors which shut off the stairs to the second floor. He pushed them open, cast a cool expressionless glance

up and down the street, and moved inside. If he had been a smaller man and more quietly dressed, I might have thought he was going to pull a stick-up. But not in those clothes, and not with that hat, and that frame.

The doors swung back outwards and almost settled to a stop. Before they had entirely stopped moving they opened again, violently, outwards. Something sailed across the sidewalk and landed in the gutter between two parked cars. It landed on its hands and knees and made a high keening noise like a cornered rat. It got up slowly, retrieved a hat and stepped back on to the sidewalk. It was a thin, narrow-shouldered brown youth in a lilac coloured suit and a carnation. It had slick black hair. It kept its mouth open and whined for a moment. People stared at it vaguely. Then it settled its hat jauntily, sidled over to the wall and walked silently splay-footed off along the block.

Silence. Traffic resumed. I walked along to the double doors and stood in front of them. They were motionless now. It wasn't any of my business. So I pushed them open and looked in.

Read the extract again. Then write down everything which suggests that it's written by an American and set in America.

This last activity, although interesting, is a bit dangerous if it leaves you with the idea that American writing is all like Raymond Chandler. It isn't. American writing is wonderfully varied. To end with, here is a poem by Theodore Roethke, whose father's family came to America from Germany. The poem is called *The Storm*, and describes a rising storm in an Italian seaside town. You don't have to do anything *with* this poem. Just read it.

The Storm

Against the stone breakwater,
Only an ominous lapping,
While the wind whines overhead,
Coming down from the mountain,
Whistling between the arbours, the winding
    terraces;

A thin whine of wires, a rattling and
    flapping of leaves,
And the small streetlamp swinging and
    slamming against the lamp-pole.
Where have the people gone?
There is one light on the mountain.
Along the sea-wall a steady sloshing of the
    swell,
The waves not yet high, but even,
Coming closer and closer upon each other;
A fine fume of rain driving in from the sea,
Riddling the sand, like a wide spray of
    buckshot,
The wind from the sea and the wind from the
    mountain contending,
Flicking the foam from the whitecaps
    straight upwards into the darkness.
A time to go home!
And a child's dirty shift billows upward out
    of an alley;
A cat runs from the wind as we do,
Between the whitening trees, up Santa
    Lucia.

Where the heavy door unlocks
And our breath comes more easy.
Then a crack of thunder, and the black rain
    runs over us, over
The flat-roofed houses, coming down in
    gusts, beating
The walls, the slatted windows, driving
The last watcher indoors, moving the
    cardplayers closer
To their cards, their Lachryma Christi.
We creep to our bed and its straw mattress.
We wait, we listen.
The storm lulls off, then redoubles,
Bending the trees halfway down to the
    ground,
Shaking loose the last wizened oranges in
    the orchard,
Flattening the limber carnations.
A spider eases himself down from a swaying
    light bulb,
Running over the coverlet, down under the
    iron bedstead.
The bulb goes on and off, weakly.
Water roars in the cistern.
We lie closer on the gritty pillow,
Breathing heavily, hoping—
For the last great leap of the wave over the
    breakwater,
The flat boom on the beach of the towering
    sea-swell,
The sudden shudder as the jutting sea-cliff
    collapses
And the hurricane drives the dead straw
    into the living pine-tree.

Lachryma Christi—a drink

****

There we'll leave America, and this chapter, and this book. Although a lot has gone into the book, a lot has been missed out as well. The language of television, of newspapers, of advertising, of male and female roles; we have said little or nothing about them. They are important kinds of language, and really deserve a book to themselves. We hope that you have found at least some of the ideas and activities in this book interesting and worthwhile.

One thought: language is bound up with the fates and histories of the people who speak it. When they change, their language changes too.